EASY STEPS FOR

Better Health

God's plan for a balanced and more fulfilling life.

D0802245

by SHAWN BOONSTRA
with Fred Hardinge, DrPH, RD

IT IS WRITTEN
INTERNATIONAL TELEVISION

and Pacific Press Publishing Association

Design and Layout by Fred Knopper
Editing by Judy Knopper and Kari Kurti
Photo credit: www.photos.com

Copyright 2007 by It Is Written. All Rights Reserved.

Additional copies of this book are available by
calling toll free 1-888-664-5573 or visiting
www.itiswritten.com

Unless otherwise noted, all Bible texts are from the
New King James Version, copyright 1979, 1980, 1982
by Thomas Nelson, Inc. Used by permission.

Portions of this book have been previously
published in *To Your Health,* by Shawn Boonstra,
It Is Written, Canada, March 2003.

Printed in the United States of America
by Pacific Press Publishing Association
Nampa, Idaho / Oshawa, Ontario, Canada
www.pacificpress.com

ISBN 10: 0816322007
ISBN 13: 9780816322008

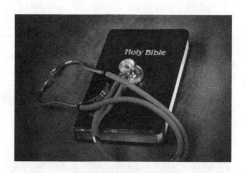

PLEASE NOTE

The information in this book can lead to better health. However, as valuable as this may be, it is not intended to take the place of a qualified physician, and cannot be considered a substitute for sound medical advice. You are advised to consult a qualified health practitioner for the treatment of medical problems or before making significant lifestyle changes. Never stop taking medication or treatment without consulting your physician.

"If you diligently heed the voice
of the LORD your God
and do what is right in His sight,
give ear to His commandments
and keep all His statutes,
I will put none of the diseases
on you which I have brought
on the Egyptians.
For I am the LORD who heals you."

EXODUS 15:26

Contents

Beloved, I pray that you may
prosper in all things and
be in health.

3 JOHN 2

CHAPTER ONE

Introduction

It's About More Than Living Longer

A few years ago I (Fred Hardinge[1]) was greeting people after preaching in a church I was visiting when a lady walked up and said, "Pastor, I have a question for you. Do you believe Jesus is coming soon?" I looked at her and replied, "Of course I do. He is coming very soon!"

Then with much passion she exclaimed, "In that case, why are you so concerned about all this health business? It won't make any difference if I live and eat as I choose, because Christ is going to come before I die, and my Bible says that I will be changed in the twinkling of an eye. So I don't have to worry about these things!" And she walked out of the church. Since then, I have done a lot of thinking about that short conversation.

Today, science tells us that by making healthy choices we have a much better chance of living longer. There's really no question about that fact. The literature is replete with study after study highlighting the value of wise choices in the area of health. But is that the primary reason Christians should make careful choices in their lifestyle? Consider that as we make healthy choices and live longer and better, we also think better!

John F. Kennedy is reported to have once quoted from the ancient Greeks, saying:

Physical fitness is not only one of the most important keys to a healthy body, it is the basis of dynamic and creative intellectual activity. Intelligence and skill can only function at the peak of their capacity when the body is healthy and strong; hardy spirits and tough minds usually inhabit sound bodies.[2]

Both the Old and New Testaments are rich in principles, even rules, for both physical and emotional health. The apostle Paul gave a special impetus to the importance of following health principles when he wrote:

Or do you not know that your body is the temple of the Holy Spirit who is in you, whom you have from God, and you are not your own? For you were bought at a price; therefore glorify God in your body and in your spirit, which are God's. (1 Corinthians. 6:19, 20)

What is Paul implying here in this passage? In Corinth there were many, many temples to their idols. It was a heathen, Gentile city. No doubt some of those attracted to Paul's preaching were wondering where his temple was located. There was a temple in Jerusalem but not one in Corinth. So he was really saying, "You don't need a temple. *You* are the temple of the Holy Spirit."

The ability for us to think is a physiological function of our brain, and is dependent on all the body's support systems to keep it functioning and sharp. Paul informs us that the human body is designed to be the abode of God's divine Spirit. God desires to dwell within us. Not only does he daily give us life, He also gives us the privilege of inviting Him to control the processes of our life and that which results from it.

A few years ago I (Fred Hardinge) was looking for a used car. After studying the classifieds carefully, and making a number of phone calls, I located two good possibilities that were in my price range and made arrangements to go see them. When I drove up to the first address I couldn't believe my eyes. The car in the driveway with the "For Sale" sign looked as new and pristine as when it was driven from the showroom. It was shiny and bright without any scratches—and the interior looked and smelled brand new. After talking with the owner for a few minutes, I asked him if I could see the service records of this vehicle. At that he laughed and said, "This car is so good that I have not had to have it serviced for over 60,000 miles. I've never even had to change the oil!" It was really tempting to buy this car on the spot, but I had to go see the other vehicle.

When I drove to the second home, there was the identical model in the driveway, but it didn't look as clean and new as the first one. And, this owner was asking a few more dollars for his car than the previous one. This car had some parking-lot dings in the finish. The interior was good, but it looked like it had been used for 60,000-plus miles. I asked the owner the same question about service records. He excused himself, went into the house and returned with all the service receipts neatly organized.

Which car did I purchase? Of course, the one that was faithfully serviced. Today, a dozen years later, I am still driving that car. It now has nearly 300,000 miles on it, and has not given me any trouble. It is the most inexpensive car I have ever owned.

Being biologically irresponsible internally is just as much a disgrace to God as to have the outside of the body coated with filth. Yet, too often we keep the outward adorning clean, but the inside is a mess! Remember what Jesus said to the Pharisees:

"Woe to you, scribes and Pharisees, hypocrites! For you are like whitewashed tombs which indeed appear beautiful outwardly, but inside are full of dead men's bones and all uncleanness." (Matthew 23:27)

If we are truly the temple of God and His Spirit, then certainly we should keep things internally neat and tidy. Living in harmony with God's laws, physiologically, best accomplishes this.

There are those who sometimes think that harmony with Biblical principles sucks all of the joy out of life. I remember someone who was told that he would live longer if he quit drinking, smoking and carousing. "Will I really live longer," he asked sarcastically, "or will it just *feel* that way?"

It's hard for some people to imagine that clean living is also enjoyable living. I can personally assure you that if you follow the Bible's advice, not only will you live longer, you will also enjoy life more. Honest! Look at what Jesus says on the subject:

"The thief does not come except to steal, and to kill, and to destroy. I have come that they may have life, and that they may have it more abundantly." (John 10:10)

God does not want to ruin your life—He wants to improve it. Many advertisers try to sell us the good life, but having witnessed firsthand some of the consequences of their value system, I'm not convinced they understand what the good life really is.

On the other hand, God does understand, and He is uniquely qualified to comment on the subject. The Creator is able to see the big picture. He knows the end from the beginning. He understands exactly how you are wired, because He designed you. There is more to life than just living longer.

We are all familiar with the prediction in Isaiah 7:14 that Jesus would be born to a virgin. However, we rarely look at the next verse:

"Curds and honey He shall eat, that He may know to refuse the evil and choose the good." (Isaiah 7:15)

The phrase, "curds and honey" (or "butter and honey"), is a symbol in Scripture of adequacy and plenty. God described the land He chose for His people as one filled with "milk and honey," a land that had everything they needed including adequate nutrition. Isaiah states in this verse that the coming Savior would eat this good food that He might have clear thoughts to "refuse the evil and choose the good."

The prophet Isaiah also describes God's communication to us when he wrote:

Your ears shall hear a word behind you, saying, "This is the way, walk in it, whenever you turn to the right hand or whenever you turn to the left." (Isaiah 30:21)

The only way God communicates with us is through our mind, which is our brain. We have special senses that connect us to our internal and external environment. You are reading this book using your sense of sight. You watch television using your eyes and ears. These senses allow you to perceive what is going on right here and now. The only access the Holy Spirit has to our minds is through our senses, which have been called the avenues of the soul.

The devil also can use these senses. He is well aware that God communicates to us through these avenues. If you were the devil, wouldn't you want to blunt these avenues in order to still God's voice in our minds?

Unhealthful practices in thinking, eating and living make God's voice of instruction and direction less distinct. Our minds become clouded. Perhaps it is because we do not get physical exercise. It may be because we eat excessively. Or maybe we don't sleep enough and our brains are so wearied that our decision-making capacity is weakened. And, of course, there are those who take various chemicals into their bodies that fog the thinking mechanisms.

All this is just what the devil wants. In this condition we may not hear the voice of the Holy Spirit saying, "This is the way, walk ye in it." The Lord doesn't shout at us. He uses a still, small voice when providing us direction.

Unfortunately, our minds are often inefficient because we disregard biological laws and thus cannot perceive God's will as clearly as God desires. The battle for our soul is really the battle for control of our minds. God has provided wise instruction in His Word which, when followed, will not simply help us live longer, but will help us more clearly hear His gentle voice speaking to us.

Our physiology is not beyond the intellectual grasp of God. He has a complete set of blueprints, for He is the Master Craftsman. He holds the secret of life. He adds the divine spark to organic material that causes it to live, breathe and think. As valuable as modern science is, it will never be able to accomplish that.

It is our prayer that as you explore this book you will discover important aspects of the Creator's plan for balancing your physical, spiritual and mental health. While the information presented on the subject is hardly exhaustive, it is our desire that, as you read, you may experience the joys of hearing God's voice speaking to you.

I will praise You, for I am fearfully and wonderfully made; Marvelous are Your works, and that my soul knows very well. My frame was not hidden from You, when I was made in secret, and skillfully wrought in the lowest parts of the earth. Your eyes saw my substance, being yet unformed. And in Your book they all were written, the days fashioned for me, when as yet there were none of them. (Psalm 139:14-16)

No wonder people who follow the Designer's advice enjoy life more—and have more life to enjoy!

---

[1] Both Shawn Boonstra and Fred Hardinge contributed to the content of this book. Unless otherwise noted, personal stories and pronouns refer to Pastor Boonstra.
[2] As quoted on http://www.internationalsport.com/nsd/nsd_quotes.cfm.

CHAPTER TWO

The Bible and Health

How to Postpone Your Funeral

Read the Bible carefully and you might notice something striking: *God doesn't like funerals!* Funerals were never part of His original plan. We weren't supposed to die. God made dirt for growing fruits and vegetables; He did not make dirt for covering up corpses or propping up tombstones.

Perhaps that's why God seems to be in the business of breaking up funerals. For example, through the ministry of the prophet Elijah, He raised a widow's son from the dead (1 Kings 17:22). Through the ministry of Paul, God resurrected a young man who fell asleep during the sermon and fell from a window to his death (Acts 20:9, 10). Through the ministry of Peter, He rescued the much-loved and sorely missed Dorcas from death's icy grip (Acts 9:36-42).

When the Son of God Himself walked the earth, He literally broke up a funeral when He raised a window's son from the dead (Luke 7:15). He also brought back Jairus' daughter (Mark 5:41, 42), and called His good friend Lazarus out of the grave after he had been dead for four days (John 11:43, 44). And when Jesus Himself died at Calvary, the Bible tells us:

And graves were opened; and many bodies of the saints who had fallen asleep were raised; and coming out of the graves after His resurrection, they went into the holy city and appeared to many. (Matthew 27:52, 53)

The crowning proof, of course, that God loves to break up a funeral is found in the fact that He raised His own Son from the dead. And, because He did that, you and I will one day come out of our graves when Christ returns (John 5:28; 1 Thessalonians 4:13-17; 1 Corinthians 15:51-55). Death, says the Bible, will one day be "swallowed up in victory" (1 Corinthians 15:54).

The Bible couldn't be more clear: *God hates death.* He also hates everything that causes it—including disease. A quick glance at the ministry of Jesus proves it:

Then Jesus went about all the cities and villages, teaching in their synagogues, preaching the gospel of the kingdom, and healing every sickness and every disease among the people. (Matthew 9:35)

There are two things you will typically find Jesus doing with His time on earth: (1) preaching and teaching, and (2) healing the sick. Some Bible students have estimated that Jesus spent more time healing people than He did preaching to them. Interesting!

The stories of Jesus' ministry are particularly revealing of His love for humanity. When a leper came to Jesus and asked to be healed, Jesus was "moved with compassion" and healed him (Mark 1:41). As the Creator, He knew that the leper wasn't originally designed to be a leper and suffer. On another occasion, when Jesus saw a large crowd of diseased people it tore at His heart. He was "moved with compassion" the Bible tells us, and healed every last one of them (Matthew 14:14). On still another occasion, He encountered two blind men sitting by the road. He knew that their darkened eyes had been created to witness God's loving glory in creation, not to be wasted in idle darkness. He couldn't bear it. He restored their sight (Matthew 9:27-30).

The testimony of the Bible is clear: God doesn't like death, and He certainly doesn't like disease. Yet some Christians—to listen to them—seem to think that God is not the least bit interested in our physical well-being. I've heard Christians say things that make me think their best impression of God is that He is only interested in the "great hereafter."

Nothing could be further from the truth. I believe that this kind of erroneous thinking is, at least in part, the result of our tendency to divide our existence into two separate compartments: the spiritual and the physical. We come by this tendency honestly; we have our philosophical heritage to thank for it. The ancient Greeks had a dualistic view of the world, dividing all existence into separate physical and spiritual realms. The philosopher Plato, in particular, taught something that modern students of philosophy refer to as the *Theory of Forms*.

Plato's *Theory of Forms* teaches that the world we perceive with our five senses (sight, hearing, touch, taste and smell) is imperfect and therefore flawed. The only way we know it's flawed is because we have an idea of what perfection might be like. Plato concluded that the *physical* world we detect with our senses is, therefore, an imperfect representation of a perfect *spiritual* world that exists somewhere "out there."

Students of philosophy have illustrated Plato's theory in a number of ways. For example, in mathematics a "line" is something that has infinite length but virtually no breadth. It is considered to be just a single point wide. That's why you were taught to draw a "line" in math class like this:

This "line" has an arrow at each end to represent the fact that it continues on forever in both directions. It is infinitely long, but only one point wide. The problem with drawing a line is that nothing you can draw with a pencil will ever be only one point wide (or for that matter, infinitely long). Nothing is smaller than a point, because it is theoretically indivisible. Your pencil lead is *much* wider than a point.

Plato might argue, then, that your drawing is an imperfect representation of a line, because no matter how thin you draw it, it will never be just one point wide or infinitely long. Your best efforts to draw a line still have some width to them and are limited in length. It is, therefore, just a symbol or "form," not a *real* mathematical line. (Of course, real lines exist; we just can't draw them.)

I know it may seem like we are splitting hairs, but this is an important concept because it has literally altered the way the whole Western World thinks. Plato argued that everything around us is a "form" of something better in the spiritual realm. Nothing we see is real. A chair is not a real chair; it is merely a "form" of the "ideal" chair in the spiritual ream.

Here is another popular illustration of Plato's theory. Suppose a man lives at the very back of a cave. He never leaves the cave and he cannot see the mouth. However, light from the outside world reaches the back wall and he can see the shadows of things that pass by. The shadows are not reality; they are merely "forms" of reality. Our world, argued Plato, is the back of the cave. The things we see are mere shadows of a greater reality in the spiritual realm.

Platonic Greek philosophers divided the whole universe into two realms: perfect and imperfect, or spiritual and physical. They spent most of their time trying to figure out what was real and what was merely a "form." They longed to break free of the physical world and ascend to the higher, purer plane of the spiritual world.

Dualistic thinking was also applied to the human body. Since the body is material and physical, it was believed it is merely a "form." It is therefore imperfect and of lesser value than its perfect counterpart in the spiritual realm.

This sort of thinking made its way into the Christian church where some early movements considered the human body to be inherently evil. The early ascetics,[3] for example, bodily punished themselves in an attempt to escape the sinful realities of physical existence. They denied themselves every conceivable pleasure in pursuit of holiness. Origen of Alexandria was known to sleep on the floor, walk barefoot, and go on extreme fasts. Abba Bessarion stood in the middle of a thorn bush and reportedly managed to keep himself awake for fourteen straight days. One hermit from Egypt, tempted by impure thoughts of women, punished himself by burning his fingers one by one in the flame of a lamp.[4]

This way of thinking became so popular at one point that it actually gave birth to the modern practice of priestly celibacy. As the Roman Church's influence spread through the world during the fourth and fifth centuries, her priests sought to establish themselves as spiritual authorities; but they found that in some places the ascetic monks were considered to be much holier than the priests because of their strong emphasis on physical self-denial and the suppression of natural appetites. This created a credibility problem for the priests among the people who revered the ascetics, which in turn hindered the expansion of the Roman church.

Rome attempted a two-fold approach to solve the problem. Ascetic monks were invited to become priests (and thus part of the Roman hierarchy), and priests were encouraged to become more ascetic like the monks in order to gain the favor of the people. Because the ascetics practiced celibacy, the Roman priests followed suit. Author Gary Wills describes what happened:

> One way to reduce the gap between priestly and ascetic authority was for the priests to imitate the ascetics, trying to regain lost ground by becoming celibate themselves, by fasting in the city as well as in the desert. An even quicker solution might be to co-opt the ascetics, making them priests or bishops, so people could not so easily contrast the two orders to the detriment of the priests. But the desert saints resisted this tactic. To leave the desert, to give up the utopian egalitarianism of the monasteries or the splendid isolation of the hermitages, would be a descent to the ordinary after the long struggle up onto rarified heights. It would, in Gregory Nazianzus' words, be a surrender of the ascetic's dangerous glamour for the 'drudging commerce in souls.' Athanasius had to beg the desert stars to become bishops, and he sometimes failed. When the famous monk Ammonius was summoned to take on his duty as a bishop, he sent back his left ear, and threatened to send his tongue if asked again— thus disqualifying himself for ordination.[5]

While such ascetic extremes are rare in the western world today, we still unwittingly live with the heritage of Greek dualism. Many Christians, for instance, assume that God is interested only in our spiritual welfare. The physical body is considered dispensable and ultimately unnecessary. A careful examination of the Bible, however, reveals that this is untrue. God doesn't divide our existence into two distinct compartments; on the contrary, He views us as a whole.

Adam and Eve were not ghosts. God created them with perfect physical bodies and declared them to be *very* good (Genesis 1:31). In the resurrection we will be recreated with perfect physical bodies, which we will keep for eternity (Philippians 3:20, 21). According to Scripture, we were created to be perfect in a *physical* existence.

We have, however, slipped a long way down the ladder from our original state of perfection. (Perhaps an innate sense of our fallen state has made us susceptible to dualism.) Sickness and disease now plague the human race as a result of sin, and that pains the heart of God. He can't stand to watch His children suffer, so He went to the cross and suffered Himself to put a stop to it. The Psalmist reminds us:

Bless the LORD, O my soul; And all that is within me, bless His holy name! Bless the LORD, O my soul, And forget not all His benefits: Who forgives all your iniquities, Who heals all your diseases, Who redeems your life from destruction, Who crowns you with lovingkindness and tender mercies, Who satisfies your mouth with good things, So that your youth is renewed like the eagle's. (Psalm 103:1-5)

God has a plan. He is going to eradicate disease and suffering. The world will not always be racked with sickness and suffering; we are headed back to Eden! God's promise is that "affliction will not rise up the second time" (Nahum 1:9). In heaven, the leaves of the Tree of Life will be for "the healing of the nations" (Revelation 22:2). God guarantees that He will "wipe away every tear," and "there shall be no more death, nor sorrow, nor crying, and there shall be no more pain: for the former things have passed away" (Revelation 21:4).

Clearly, our physical welfare is important to God. Not only will we be free of disease and pain after Christ returns, we are to enjoy better health while we wait. Our well-being is important to Him. Notice what the apostle John wrote: "Beloved, I pray that you may prosper in all things and be in health, just as your soul prospers" (3 John 1:2).

God is not a Greek dualist. He doesn't separate the spiritual and physical components of your life. Intimately linked to each other, they are both important to Him. One affects the other. Spiritually healthy people tend to be happier and more physically healthy. Notice the relationship between the two in the advice God gave the ancient Israelites:

"If you diligently heed the voice of the LORD your God and do what is right in His sight, give ear to His commandments and keep all His statutes, I will put none of the diseases on you which I have brought on the Egyptians. For I am the LORD who heals you." (Exodus 15:26)

Do you want to enjoy better health and postpone your funeral? Then get things right with God. You can't expect to run at peak efficiency while you're refusing to cooperate with the Designer and Maker of your body.

Please don't misunderstand what I'm saying. It's not that God punishes those who refuse Him with poor health. He is not like the petty child who takes his ball and bat home when he can't have his way. He simply won't interfere in your life unless you give Him permission, because He doesn't force His way in where He is not wanted. If you shut Him out, He won't force His blessings on you.

It only makes sense to cooperate with God, doesn't it? He not only created the world, the Bible tells us that He also holds it together (Colossians 1:16, 17). He holds *you* together. And with your cooperation He can make your life better than it has ever been. Even our food goes further with God's blessing:

"So you shall serve the LORD your God, and He will bless your bread and your water. And I will take sickness away from the midst of you." (Exodus 23:25)

Spirituality and physical health are clearly related. Those who have a genuine relationship with God get more out of life than those who do not.

There are a number of reasons for this. For one, Christians are better equipped to deal with stress, because they know that God is in control of life no matter what happens. They have Someone to talk to who genuinely understands human problems better than any human counselor, and they have an absolute guarantee that what they confess privately to Him won't be repeated all over the office or neighborhood (Hebrews 4:15). That leads to fewer ulcers and headaches!

People in a good relationship with God are also more sensitive to the Holy Spirit's voice, and therefore more likely to make wise choices in life. They regularly spend time in God's Word discerning the best path for life, and as a result end up with fewer things to regret. As a result of having studied the history of God's people, they are less likely to repeat the mistakes their forefathers made.

For these reasons and more, the first principle on the road to better health is to develop a genuine relationship with God. The second principle is exceptionally simple; so simple, in fact, that I risk insulting your intelligence by mentioning it, yet very few people actually put it into practice. Here it is:

You get out of your body what you put into it.

I told you it wasn't rocket science!

The story is told of a Portuguese monastery situated on top of a 300 foot cliff. To visit the monastery you had to get into a wicker basket attached to a long rope, and the monks would haul you up the side of the cliff. It was the only way in or out.

One day a visitor was getting ready to leave the monastery. As he climbed into the basket he took a good look at the old rope it was attached to. It was beginning to get thin in places and had many loose strands. Evidently it was very old.

"Say," he nervously asked the monk who was about to lower the basket, "how often do you fellows change this rope?"

The monk smiled as the man disappeared over the edge of the cliff. "Whenever the old one breaks!" he called.

That's bad planning, don't you think? A person really should check the rope once in a while. Ropes tend to fray and break when they're dragged up and down the side of a rocky cliff all day long. Neither can *you* expect to last very long if you drag yourself out of bed every day and bump over the sharp rocks of life without ever checking your rope. You cannot treat your body in just any way you please and still expect to get good results! Your God-given body is an amazing machine. Modern science has not been able to replicate what God has designed. No computer is as powerful as your mind, which is able to love, pray and contemplate its own existence. No mechanical device created by man is as accurate or sensitive as your hand. No camera is as good as the human eye.

Yet we sometimes treat our machines with more respect than we treat our bodies. We service our cars regularly, because they are expensive and we want them to last. We oil our tools because they're costly and we don't want them to rust. Most of the time, however, we never give our irreplaceable and finely tuned bodies a second thought.

That's a bad idea. Your body is a precision instrument that will not last forever. It requires care. Technically, you don't even own it; it belongs to Someone else. That's what the apostle Paul teaches:

Or do you not know that your body is the temple of the Holy Spirit who is in you, whom you have from God, and you are not your own?
(1 Corinthians 6:19)

Let's suppose that you own a very expensive sports car. Furthermore (and I realize this is a stretch), you are willing to loan it to me for a few months. "Be very careful with it," you warn me as you drop it off at my house, "because it's worth an absolute fortune. It's one of a kind. *Please* take good care of it."

"OK," I promise eagerly, "I'll take care of it." You hand me the keys.

Big mistake. When you come back for your car after three or four months, you make a horrible discovery. The tires are bald on the edges because I drove it too fast and cornered too hard. The once beautiful paint is covered with road salt because I drove it in the winter slush and never washed it. Even though the little label by the fuel door warned me to use only premium gasoline, I used an inferior gas, and the engine is burning dirty. On top of that, I smoked cheap cigars in it, let my kids eat in the back eat, and allowed the dog to sleep in it. It's filthy. Do you mind?

Of *course* you mind! You trusted me with a prized possession and I abused it. I esteemed it lightly, and in the process displayed a good deal of contempt for you. It's unlikely you will ever trust me again.

Most of us are quite sensitive about our personal belongings. So why is it that we think we can abuse our bodies and God won't mind? They don't belong to us; they are on loan from God, they're *very* expensive:

For you were bought at a price; therefore glorify God in your body and in your spirit, which are God's. (1 Corinthians 6:20)

The price God paid for you was beyond measure—infinite, in fact. "Glorify Me with your body," says God, "because it's a very expensive gift. It cost Me the blood of My Son, and I want you to take care of it."

What are you actually worth? It is sometimes said that you can calculate the value of something by what others are willing to pay for it. If I asked $30,000 for my used car, most people would simply laugh. If someone would offer me only $5,000 for it, I'd suddenly discover it's real value. It is only worth what someone is willing to pay for it.

Let that sink in for a moment, and then read the last verse again. Ask yourself this: what was God willing to pay for me?

The life of His only Son—that's your *real* worth! Humbling isn't it? It ought to be humbling enough to motivate us to take care of what God has blessed us with.

But how should you take care of your body? Late night television infomercials are bursting with exercise gadgets and diet plans meant to improve your heath and whip you into shape. One health guru tells you to eat more carbohydrates; another tells you to cut them out. Someone else tells you to rub special oil behind you ears, wrap yourself in Saran Wrap four times a week, or sit under a pyramid. Who is giving sound advice? What should you do?

Ignore them—that's what you should do. Read the owner's manual instead. It has been scientifically proven that people who live by the Bible's health principles will outlive the general public by up to ten years. Forget all the hocus-pocus and modern witchdoctors. The Bible works. Guaranteed.

Judge for yourself. For well over a century one particular group of people has been carefully reading and following the owner's manual— the Bible. Their health and longevity are a testimony to the Bible's wisdom. A 2005 *National Geographic* article tells it this way:

Adventists...observe the Sabbath on Saturday, socializing with other church members and enjoying a sanctuary in time that helps relieve stress. Today most Adventists follow the prescribed lifestyle—a testimony, perhaps, of the power of mixing health and religion.

From 1976 to 1988 the National Institutes of Health funded a study of 34,000 California Adventists to see whether their health-oriented lifestyle affected their life expectancy and risk of heart disease and cancer. The study found that the Adventist habit of consuming beans, soymilk, tomatoes, and other fruits lowered their risk of developing certain cancers. It also suggested that eating whole wheat bread, drinking five glasses of water a day, and, most surprisingly, consuming four servings of nuts a week reduced their risk of heart disease. And it found that not eating red meat had been helpful to avoid both cancer and heart disease.

In the end the study reached a stunning conclusion, says Gary Fraser of Loma Linda University: The average Adventist lived four to ten years longer than the average Californian. That makes the Adventists one of the nation's most convincing cultures of longevity.[6]

The first major study of this unique group, which began in 1958, has become known as the Adventist Mortality Study, a prospective study of 22,940 California Adventists. Organized at Loma Linda University, in Loma Linda, California, it entailed an intensive five-year follow-up and a more informal 25 year follow-up.

When compared with the non-Adventist population, the overall cancer mortality was just 60 percent for Adventist men and 76 percent for Adventist women. Specific types of cancer deaths were also lower. Lung cancer deaths were 79 percent lower, colorectal cancer deaths were 38 percent lower, breast cancer death rates for Adventist women were 15 percent lower, and prostate cancer death rates for Adventist men were eight percent lower.

Death from coronary heart disease among Adventist men was 33 percent less, while stroke death rates were 28 percent lower for men and 18 percent lower for women who were Adventist. When all causes of death within the two populations were compared, Adventist men had an overall death rate 33 percent lower and Adventist women had a rate 12 percent lower.[7]

Why? The reason is simple. Seventh-day Adventist Christians have a high regard for the Bible as the Word of God, and have taken its simple health principles to heart. As a result, they enjoy a higher quality of life and extended longevity as documented in more than 280 peer-reviewed scientific publications.[8]

These statistics are not mere coincidence. They come as the direct result of taking the owner's manual seriously. You can do it, too. Keep reading.

---

[3] *Asceticism* was a movement that stressed the systematic and sometimes extreme renunciation of personal desires and appetites. It often stressed a literal imitation of Christ's life and passion, with a devotion to charity.

[4] James E. Goehring, "Alone in the Desert?" *Christian History,* Fall 1999.

[5] Gary Wills, *Papal Sin* (Toronto: Doubleday, 2000), p. 135. I hesitate to quote from this volume because of its controversial nature. Much of the history he presents is informative and useful; however, some of the theories Wills derives from his study of history leave much to be desired from a biblical standpoint.

[6] Dan Beuttner, "The Secrets of Long Life," *National Geographic,* November 2005, p. 25.

[7] http://www.llu.edu/llu/health/mortality.html

[8] http://www.llu.edu/llu/health/references.html

CHAPTER THREE

Exercise

Get Movin'

It was 3:00 a.m. on a very humid, warm morning on the campus of the graduate school where I (Fred Hardinge) was teaching at the outskirts of Manila in the Philippines. Two of my master's degree students had just jumped into the car. We were on our way to the first marathon any of us had ever run. Isaac was from Ethiopia, and George was from Ghana; I was the professor from America. These two students were the only two in my exercise physiology class who had accepted an invitation to run the Manila International Marathon.

Personally, I was a bit dubious about whether Isaac and George would be able to complete the course since they had never run a race of any kind. I, at least, had run a couple of half-marathons and felt there was a chance I could finish the 26 miles. How wrong I was in that thinking. While both these young men had never run a race, they had spent their lives walking and running instead of riding in cars—unlike me in my American upbringing.

When the starting gun went off at 5:00 a.m. (it is common for marathons in the equatorial regions to begin very early to avoid the heat of the daytime sun), we surged forward with the rest of the crowd. It soon became apparent to me that I was no match for Isaac and George.

Out of respect they didn't want to run ahead of their professor, but it was clear to me that I was holding them back. I encouraged them to run on ahead but they refused. It took several more attempts before I convinced them that it was alright for them to run their best so finally they did. After jettisoning their running shoes, they disappeared into the crowd of runners ahead of me.

When I reached "the wall" with about five miles left to run, I was shocked to realize that both George and Isaac were now running on either side of me, smilingly broadly as they encouraged me to keep going. With disbelief I learned they had already crossed the finish line and had run back on the route to find me! By now my pace was pretty slow, but they stayed right with me to the finish. I had completed my first marathon, and they too completed their first—more than an hour ahead of me.

As we stood rejoicing together in the wonderful spray of water from a local fire hydrant, the verse in Proverbs 29:23 came to me: *A man's pride will bring him low, but the humble in spirit will retain honor...*

It was an important lesson. Isaac and George may never have run a race before, but their consistent performance of physical activity had prepared them to do better than I was able to do with what I had thought were strenuous bouts of exercise in an otherwise sedentary life. Never again have I thought disparagingly of the physical prowess of those who have spent their lives walking out of sheer necessity.

In my younger days if someone had asked whether physical activity or nutrition was more important for health, I would have decidedly replied "nutrition." Today the weight of research evidence points to physical activity as the single most important thing we can do to achieve and maintain health. Yet, good nutrition is also vital. The artificial choice between these two important ingredients of life is really like asking if the front or back wheel of a motorcycle is most important! Being both physically active and eating a nutritious diet are essential.

The importance of physical activity

Physical activity can provide you with many health benefits. People who enjoy participating in moderate to vigorous physical activity on a regular basis benefit by lowering their risk of developing coronary heart disease, stroke, non-insulin-dependent (type 2) diabetes mellitus, high blood pressure, and colon cancer by 30–50 percent.[9] Additionally, active people have lower premature death rates than people who are the least active.

Regular physical activity can improve health and reduce the risk of premature death in the following ways:[10]

- Reduces the risk of developing coronary heart disease (CHD) and the risk of dying from CHD
- Reduces the risk of stroke
- Reduces the risk of having a second heart attack in people who have already had one heart attack
- Lowers both total blood cholesterol and triglycerides, and increases high-density lipoproteins (HDL, or the "good" cholesterol)
- Lowers the risk of developing high blood pressure
- Helps reduce blood pressure in people who already have hypertension
- Lowers the risk of developing non-insulin-dependent (type 2) diabetes mellitus
- Reduces the risk of developing colon cancer
- Helps people achieve and maintain a healthy body weight
- Reduces feelings of depression and anxiety
- Promotes psychological well-being and reduces feelings of stress
- Helps build and maintain healthy bones, muscles, and joints[11]
- Helps older adults become stronger and better able to move about without falling or becoming excessively fatigued

Evidence shows that if you are not physically active, you are likely hurting your health. The closer we examine the health risks associated with inactivity, the more convincing it is that those who are not regularly physically active should become active. If you want to prevent disease you need to get moving!

Everyone can benefit from physical activity

The good news about regular physical activity is that everyone can benefit from it at every stage of life.[12]

Older adults. No one is too old to enjoy the benefits of regular physical activity. Evidence indicates that muscle-strengthening exercises can reduce the risk of falling and fracturing bones and can improve the ability to live independently.

Parents and children. Parents can help their children maintain a physically active lifestyle by providing encouragement and opportunities for physical activity. Families can plan outings and events that allow and encourage everyone in the family to be active.

Teenagers. Regular physical activity improves strength, builds lean muscle, and decreases body fat. Activity can build stronger bones to last a lifetime.

People trying to manage their weight. Regular physical activity burns calories while preserving lean muscle mass. Regular physical activity is a key component of any weight-loss or weight-management effort.

People with high blood pressure. Regular physical activity helps lower blood pressure.

People with physical disabilities, including arthritis. Regular physical activity can help people with chronic, disabling conditions improve their stamina and muscle strength. It also can improve psychological well-being and quality of life by increasing the ability to perform the activities of daily life.

Anyone under stress, including persons experiencing anxiety or depression. Regular physical activity improves one's mood, helps relieve depression, and increases feelings of well-being.

Physical activity does not need to be hard, painful or difficult to provide benefits. For many, the best news of all is that by participating in regular moderate-intensity activities we gain significant health benefits.

It is never too late to start an active lifestyle. No matter how long you have been inactive, how unfit you feel, or how old you are. Research now demonstrates that becoming more active through regular activity will make you healthier and improve your quality of life. There is no one who cannot benefit from becoming more active.

The US Surgeon General's recommendations on physical activity are summarized in the following table.[13] Where are you and how can you challenge yourself?

If...	Then...
You do not currently engage in regular physical activity.	You should begin by incorporating a few minutes of physical activity into each day, gradually building up to 30 minutes or more of moderate-intensity activities.
You are now active, but at less than the recommended levels.	You should strive to adopt more consistent activity: • moderate-intensity physical activity for 30 minutes or more on 5 or more days of the week, or • vigorous-intensity physical activity for 20 minutes or more on 3 or more days of the week.
You currently engage in moderate-intensity activities for at least 30 minutes on 5 or more days of the week.	You may achieve even greater health benefits by increasing the time spent or intensity of those activities.
You currently regularly engage in vigorous-intensity activities 20 minutes or more on 3 or more days of the week.	You should continue to do so.

Careful now. Most people over-estimate the amount of physical activity they get! How much are you really getting? What is the intensity of your typical exercise? Here is some information that will help guide you to decisions that will insure you are getting what you need.

How can I know the intensity of my physical activity?

Moderate-intensity activities include walking briskly, mowing the lawn, swimming for recreation, or bicycling. Technically, it is defined as any activity that burns 3.5 to 7 alories per minute (kcal/min).[14]

Vigorous-intensity activities are things like jogging, heavy yard work, swimming laps, or bicycling uphill. These activities burn more than 7 calories per minute (kcal/min).[15]

One of the simplest means of gauging your intensity is to apply what is called the "talk test." A person who is active at a *light intensity* level should be able to sing while doing the activity. One who is active at a *moderate intensity* level should be able to carry on a conversation comfortably while engaging in the activity. If a person becomes winded or too out of breath to carry on a conversation, the activity can be considered *vigorous*.

Time spent in physical activity depends on intensity

The goal is to burn a minimum of 150 calories in exercise per day, seven days per week—or a total of 1,050 calories per week. The more intense the activity, the less time you need to be engaged in the activity; the less intense, the more time engaged.[16]

Light-Intensity Activities:

- Walking slowly
- Golf: powered cart
- Swimming: slow treading
- Gardening or pruning
- Bicycling: very light effort
- Dusting or vacuuming
- Conditioning exercise, light stretching, or warm up

Moderate-Intensity Activities:

- Walking briskly
- Golf: pulling or carrying clubs
- Swimming: recreational
- Mowing lawn with power mower
- Tennis: doubles
- Bicycling 5 to 9 mph, on level terrain, or with a few hills
- Scrubbing floors or washing windows
- Strength training

Vigorous-Intensity Activities:

- Race walking, jogging, or running
- Swimming laps
- Mowing lawn with hand mower
- Tennis: singles
- Bicycling more than 10 mph, or on steep, uphill terrain
- Moving or pushing furniture
- Circuit training

Adults need a "recess" too

There are 1,440 minutes in every day. You should schedule 30 of them for physical activity!

Now that you know how important physical activity is for you and your health, what are you going to do about it? With a little creativity and planning, even the person with the busiest schedule can make room for physical activity. For many people, there is often available time to cycle, walk or play before or after work or meals. Think about your weekly or daily schedule, and look for or make opportunities to be more active. Every little bit helps. Consider the following suggestions:

- Walk, cycle, jog, skate etc. to work, school, the store, or place of worship.
- Park the car farther away from your destination.

- Get on or off the bus several blocks away from your destination.
- Take the stairs instead of the elevator or escalator.
- Play with children or pets—everybody wins. (If you find it too difficult to be active after work, try it before work.)
- Take fitness breaks by walking or doing desk exercises.
- Perform gardening or home repair activities.
- Avoid labor-saving devices; turn off the self-propel option on your lawn mower or vacuum cleaner.
- Use leg power; take small trips on foot to get your body moving.
- Exercise while watching TV. For example: use hand weights, stationary bicycle/treadmill/stair climber, or stretch.
- Keep a pair of comfortable walking or running shoes in your car and office. You'll be ready for activity wherever you are!
- Make a morning walk a habit.
- Walk while doing errands.

The most important thing is to incorporate physical activity into as many of your daily activities as possible.

If you have been inactive for a while (months or years), use a sensible approach by starting out slowly. You may want to choose moderate-intensity activities you enjoy the most. Gradually build up the time you spend doing the activity until you can comfortably perform it 30 minutes per day. As the minimum amount becomes easier, gradually increase the length of time or the intensity of the activity—or both. Explore new physical activities; you may discover one you enjoy more!

Avoid activity-induced injury

Some might be tempted to remain sedentary and inactive to avoid injury. However, they will then suffer the considerable risks associated with being couch potatoes. Just a little common sense will prevent most injuries associated with being active. Begin by listening to you body. Monitor your level of fatigue and physical discomfort. Breathlessness and muscle soreness could be danger signs. Be aware of dizziness and lightheadedness. Start at an easy pace and increase time or distance gradually. Use appropriate equipment and clothing for your chosen activity. Don't forget to drink enough water to replace fluids lost in perspiration (this usually means at least eight 10-ounce cups per day). If you have questions or difficulties, be sure to consult your personal physician.

Overcome the barriers to physical activity

If physical activity is so important to achieving and maintaining good health, why do two out of three Americans fail to be active at recommended levels? Understanding the common barriers to physical activity can help you become more active and enjoy the enormous benefits discussed in this chapter. There are many personal barriers to being active including physiological, behavioral and psychological. The 10 most common reasons adults give for not adopting a more physically active lifestyle are:[17]

1. Do not have enough time to exercise
2. Find it inconvenient to exercise
3. Lack self-motivation
4. Do not find exercise enjoyable
5. Find exercise boring
6. Lack confidence in their ability to be physically active (low self-efficacy)
7. Fear being injured or have been injured recently
8. Lack self-management skills, such as the ability to set personal goals, monitor progress, or reward progress toward such goals
9. Lack encouragement, support, or companionship from family and friends, and
10. Do not have parks, sidewalks, bicycle trails, or safe and pleasant walking paths convenient to their homes or offices.

Which barriers affect you the most?

Chances are that with some careful and creative thought you can discover ways to overcome them.

Rounding out your activity program with strength training

Scientific research has shown that physical activity can slow the physiological aging clock. While aerobic exercise, such as walking, jogging or swimming, has many excellent health benefits—it maintains the heart and lungs and increases cardiovascular fitness and endurance—it does not make your muscles strong. Strength training does. Studies have shown that lifting weights two or three times a week increases strength by building muscle mass and bone density. Strength training in conjunction with other physical activities can have a profound impact on increasing your strength, and maintaining the integrity of your bones, as well as improving your balance, coordination and mobility. In addition, strength training can help reduce the signs and symptoms of many chronic diseases, including arthritis.

There are many excellent strength training programs available today in books, videos and gyms. I would like to recommend one that is free to anyone who has access to the Internet. It was developed by Tufts University in conjunction with the Centers for Disease Control. If you are not in the "older" generation, please don't let the title put you off. This program is valuable for adults of all ages. Online guides[18] are available with short videos, downloadable record sheets and illustrations. If you would rather be guided by a downloadable book, you may get a printer-friendly version *of Growing Stronger—Strength Training for Older Adults.*[19] By following either version you will be healthier and stronger.

Conclusion

Today we benefit from many of the technological advances of the modern era. With the myriad labor-saving devices available we have become increasingly sedentary—and suffer accordingly. Our great-grandparents really didn't have to carve out time in their lifestyles to get physical activity. Almost everything they did was physical! Most of us, however, must be very intentional about getting the physical activity we need.

When God created humans in the Garden of Eden He intended that we get physical activity. *Then the LORD God took the man and put him in the garden of Eden to tend and keep it* (Genesis 2:15). Anyone who knows about farming understands it is a lifestyle filled with physical activity.

If you are having trouble sleeping, remember the words of Solomon in Ecclesiastes 5:12: *The sleep of a laboring man is sweet...* There is probably no better sleeping pill (with no negative side-effects!) than regular physical activity.

We can't roll back the clock of progress, and we certainly don't want to forgo using the advantages of modern technology. However, if we plan to enjoy these blessings for a long time, we must find the time to regularly engage in good physical activity as described in this chapter. It is a matter of choice. We have to "get movin'!"

(As I finish writing this chapter I realize I have been sitting in front of my computer for several hours. I must put my coat on and go for a walk now...)[20]

---

[9] USDHHS, Physical Activity Fundamental To Preventing Disease, June 20, 2002.

[10] http://www.cdc.gov/nccdphp/dnpa/physical/importance/why.htm

[11] Kanis, J. A. et al. Long-term risk of osteoporotic fracture in Malmo. Osteoporosis International, 2000; 11:669-674.

[12] Pate, R. R., Pratt, M., Blair, S. N., et al. Physical activity and public health: a recommendation from the Centers for Disease Control and Prevention and the American College of Sports Medicine. *Journal of the American Medical Association* 1995;273(5):402-407.

[13] http://www.cdc.gov/nccdphp/dnpa/physical/recommendations/adults.htm

[14] Ainsworth, B. E., Haskell, W. L., Leon, A. S., et al. Compendium of physical activities: classification of energy costs of human physical activities. *Medicine and Science in Sports and Exercise* 1993; 25(1):71–80.

[15] Ibid.

[16] For a more detailed look at the intensity of various activities visit: http://www.cdc.gov/nccdphp/dnpa/physical/pdf/PA_Intensity_table_2_1.pdf

[17] Sallis, J. F., Hovell, M. F. Determinants of exercise behavior. *Exercise and Sport Science Reviews* 1990;18:307-330.

[18] http://www.cdc.gov/nccdphp/dnpa/physical/growing_stronger/index.htm

[19] http://www.cdc.gov/nccdphp/dnpa/physical/growing_stronger/resources.htm

[20] Fred Hardinge was the primary contributor to this chapter on exercise.

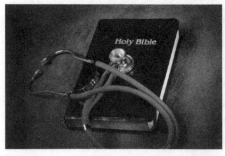

CHAPTER FOUR

Diet

Why Mozart Died Young

In the beginning God created man—then He gave him a menu. What was on it?

And God said, "See, I have given you every herb that yields seed which is on the face of all the earth, and every tree whose fruit yields seed; to you it shall be for food." (Genesis 1:29)

Read the verse again carefully. It was a *vegetarian* menu. Adam and Eve never chased a cow through the forests of Paradise with a knife. There were no slaughterhouses. Death was unknown in the Garden of Eden. The first human beings were vegetarian by design.

The diet God originally chose for us did not include the flesh of animals. How could there have been killing of animals in that perfect environment of Eden?

Doctors and nutritionists today are continually reminding us to cut down on the amount of animal fats we consume because the high cholesterol levels produced from eating these items are killing us. We suffer from affluent lifestyle diseases that were relatively unknown to our forefathers.

Even our governments are getting involved in delivering this message. Recently you may have been trying to eat right by working to

fit the "5 A Day" program into your life—that is, five or more servings
of fruits and vegetables each day. Well, the government now has some
news for you: Forget five a day—more is better. Starting in March
2007, the Centers for Disease Control and the Produce for Better Health
Foundation are launching a national campaign with the message, "*Fruits
& Veggies—More Matters*."

The new slogan replaces the old "5 A Day" campaign, which dates
back to the early 1990s. The reason? Under the U.S. government's latest
food guidelines, five servings of fruits and vegetables may not be enough.
Adults need anywhere from seven to 13 servings of produce daily to get
all the health benefits fruits and vegetables provide.

There is plenty of scientific evidence to document the health benefits
of a diet rich in fruits and vegetables, like the original diet in Eden.
Fruits and veggies are brimming with disease-fighting phytochemicals,
antioxidants, vitamins, minerals, fiber, water, complex carbohydrates,
and a good share of protein. Not only that, they're naturally low in
sodium and calories, cholesterol-free and virtually fat-free.

A balanced diet rich in fruits and vegetables may be your best defense
against obesity, heart disease, type 2 diabetes, certain cancers and other
chronic diseases. It is important to eat a rainbow of colored fruits and
vegetables every day. The pigments found in produce act as antioxidants,
helping to rid your body of "free radicals" that can damage cells.

With more than two-thirds of American adults overweight, the
weight-control benefits of fruits and veggies are especially important.
The high amount of fiber and water in fruits and vegetables contribute
to the sensation of feeling full, thus preventing overeating. And the
substitution of lower calorie fruits and vegetables for "empty calorie"
foods that offer little nutritional value can really make a difference. In
addition, the nutrition provided by fruits and vegetables will simply help
you feel better.

Adam didn't have cholesterol problems and quite likely did not die
of a heart attack or stroke. If he were still alive today, he would have
virtually no risk as a vegetarian of getting mad cow disease, trichinosis,
E. coli poisoning, or any of the other modern diseases associated with
eating contaminated flesh food.[21]

It wasn't until after the Great Flood that God gave us explicit permission to eat meat.[22] It's always possible that somebody got the idea to kill and eat animals before that time, but you won't find any record of God sanctioning it prior to Noah's time.[23] The change in diet came with good cause. When Noah and his family climbed out of the ark onto a flood-scarred planet, there wasn't a lot of broccoli or spinach available. The animals on the ark were likely about the only thing immediately available for lunch.

When God gave Noah license to eat flesh, however, it was still not blanket permission to eat anything he might want. Only "clean" animals were fit for food; others were off limits for consumption.

"Wait a minute!" someone occasionally protests. "The distinction between clean and unclean animals was only for the Jews." Not according to the Bible. Noah predates the existence of the Jewish nation by hundreds of years, and yet Noah clearly knew the difference between clean and unclean animals. Consider the biblical evidence:

Then the LORD said to Noah, "Come into the ark, you and all your household, because I have seen that you are righteous before Me in this generation. You shall take with you seven each of every clean animal, a male and his female; two each of animals that are unclean, a male and his female;" (Genesis 7:1, 2)

Almost 1,000 years before Moses and the Jews,[24] Noah knew the difference. As a boy, I learned that Noah took two of each animal into the ark. This is only partially true; Noah took two of each unclean animal onto the ark, but he took seven of each clean animal. The distinction between clean and unclean animals predates the Jewish nation by a very long time. God is not arbitrary; He forbids the consumption of unclean animals for a very good reason. *They aren't good for you!* Statistically, those who avoid them can expect to live a number of years longer that those who eat them.[25]

How do you tell the difference between clean and unclean animals? It's quite simple. Many centuries after Noah, the Jews left us a record of God's specific instructions:

"Among the animals, whatever divides the hoof, having cloven hooves and chewing the cud—that you may eat." (Leviticus 11:3)

A clean land animal has two distinctive characteristics: it chews the cud and has a cloven hoof. If both of these characteristics are present, the animal is fit to eat. The list of clean animals includes cows, moose, deer lamb, goat and a number of other North American favorites. If an animal does not chew the cud *and* have a cloven hoof, however, it is considered unclean.

"Nevertheless these you shall not eat among those that chew the cud or those that have cloven hooves: the camel, because it chews the cud but does not have cloven hooves, is unclean to you; the rock hyrax, because it chews the cud but does not have cloven hooves, is unclean to you; 'the hare, because it chews the cud but does not have cloven hooves, is unclean to you;" (Leviticus 11:4-6)

"But rabbit (hare) tastes *sooooo* good!" someone protests. I'll be the first to admit that's true. When I was a boy I thought rabbit was delicious. The Bible doesn't argue the fact that many unclean animals taste good. Consider this, however: if they didn't taste good, God would not waste time warning us not to eat them. We simply would never be tempted. God warns us precisely because they *do* taste good.

Rabbit simply isn't good for you. They tend to overpopulate and consequently carry a lot of disease. I have seen survival manuals that advise against eating rabbit meat when you're lost in the woods because you could end up with a case of diarrhea that might kill you. When God warns you not to eat rabbit, He is not trying to ruin a tasty meal; He is literally trying to save your life!

There is more on the Bible's list of unclean animals:

"...and the swine, though it divides the hoof, having cloven hooves, yet does not chew the cud, is unclean to you. Their flesh you shall not eat, and their carcasses you shall not touch. They are unclean to you." (Leviticus 11:7, 8)

Ouch. Not everybody in our western culture enjoys eating rabbit, but pork products are wildly popular. Bacon, ham and sausage are all tasty and relatively inexpensive. However, the Bible prohibits eating them.

Let's ask an interesting historical question that may throw a little light on the subject. What killed Mozart? According to a 2001 article published in the Archives of Internal Medicine, it was probably a pig.

"Forget rheumatic fever, kidney stones, heart disease, pneumonia and even poisoning. What really killed Wolfgang Amadeus Mozart 210 years ago could have been pork cutlets."

The principle author of this article,[26] Dr. Jan V. Hirschmann of Puget Sound Veterans Affairs Medical Center in Seattle, suggests the latest theory about Mozart's untimely death in Vienna on Dec 5, 1791 at age 35 was likely trichinosis. This is a parasitic infestation that is usually caused by eating undercooked pork. It is often associated with all of the symptoms Mozart had, which included fever, rash, limb pain and swelling.

In 1846, years after Mozart's death, Dr. Joseph Leidy of Philadelphia was eating a slice of ham for lunch when he noticed some funny-looking spots in it. He thought, "Those spots look familiar. I saw those very same spots in the muscle tissue of a corpse I was dissecting the other day!" (I hope you have got a strong stomach!)

He took his ham and put it under a microscope. What he discovered was truly horrifying—it was full of tiny little worms we now call Trichina. Trichina worms work their way into your muscles, and can eventually kill you. In human beings they come almost exclusively from eating pork products. The pigs we eat acquire the worms from eating garbage and other unsavory items.

Mozart wrote a letter to his wife 44 days before his mysterious illness began: "What do I smell…pork cutlets? Che Gusto (what a delicious taste)! I eat to your health."[27]

He ate to his wife Constanze's health, perhaps, but tragically not to his own. Mozart died 15 days after he became ill. He had written the letter 44 days before he got sick. Trichinosis has an incubation period of around 50 days. Dr. Hirschmann points out that the timing was right and Mozart's symptoms were strikingly similar to what happens when people eat parasite-infested pork.

What types of symptoms could you expect if you ingested trichina? A rather descriptive *Reader's Digest* article from half a century ago spells it out:

A single serving of infective pork, even a single mouthful,

can kill or cripple or condemn the victim to a lifetime of aches and pins. For this unique disease, trichinosis, there is no cure. With no drug to stop them, the worms may spread through the muscular tissues of the entire human system. One of two things then happens, depending on the intensity of the infection. Either death ensues or a successful effort is made by nature to throw an enclosure, or cyst around each of the teeming parasites, which then become dormant although they remain alive for years...Trichinosis can simulate in some degree almost any other malady. Physicians have confused trichinosis with some 50 ailments, ranging from typhoid fever to acute alcoholism. That pain in your arm or leg may be arthritis or rheumatism, but it may be trichinosis: That pain in your back may mean a gall-bladder involvement, but it may mean trichinosis.[28]

Another description comes to us courtesy of the United States Department of Agriculture:

If the initial infection is relatively heavy, a person may have an upset stomach, vomiting, diarrhea and other symptoms within 24 to 48 hours. However, these symptoms are often absent.

The symptoms characteristically associated with trichinosis occur during the period of migration and encystment. This starts about a week after infection and may continue for a month or more. When thousands of young trichinae travel though the body at one time, the person may have muscular pain, rising fever, headache and prostration. When the larvae reach the muscles, other symptoms develop. These include swelling of the face and other parts of the body, sore eyes, hemorrhages, fever and difficult breathing. Stiffness of the muscles may occur in severe infections. Some patients may have symptoms of heart disease or symptoms of brain disorder, such as delirium or coma.[29]

Some have pointed out that we get trichinosis only from eating undercooked pork. This is largely true. However, as medical doctor Don Colbert points out:

> ...cooking pork at temperatures of 160 degrees Fahrenheit or greater will kill the parasites, but it should be noted that the center portion of pork steaks or pork chops must be heated to this temperature or parasites will not be killed. Often this does not occur.[30]

There are regulations to deal with these sorts of problems, but they are not always as stringent as we might hope. The USDA article previously cited notes that, "an arbitrary figure of one or more larvae per gram generally has been accepted as the infection level at which some danger to human health might be present. Conversely pork infected with fewer that one larva per gram is generally not likely to be harmful to humans."[31] One gram of pork is about the size of a lima bean. In four ounces of pork you would have to find more than 112 worms before the meat was considered unfit for sale!

According to the Centers for Disease Control, this infection used to be very common and was caused by eating undercooked pork:

> However, infection is now relatively rare. During 1997-2001, an average of 12 cases per year were reported. The number of cases has decreased because of legislation prohibiting the feeding of raw-meat garbage to hogs, commercial and home freezing of pork, and the public awareness of the danger of eating raw or undercooked pork products. Cases are less commonly associated with pork products and more often associated with eating raw or undercooked wild game meats.[32]

It should be noted here that although flesh foods other than pork and wild game are unlikely to contain trichinella, all flesh foods must be cooked to adequate temperatures to be safe from all harmful bacteria.

This includes minimum internal temperatures for pork, ground beef and egg dishes of 160°F, and all poultry of 165°F. Beef roasts and fish are safe at 145°F.[33]

In addition to parasites, there are other problems with pork. Dr. Colbert sums up the problems in his book, *What Would Jesus Eat?* as follows:

> Many people declare today that pork is a safe meat to eat in modern times. I disagree. Pigs eat enormous amounts of food, and this dilutes the hydrochloric acid in a pig's stomach. This in turn allows toxins, viruses, parasites, and bacteria to be absorbed into the animal's flesh. Besides being gluttons, swine are also extremely filthy animals. They will eat garbage, feces, and even decaying flesh. Pigs readily harbor parasites including Trichinella, the pork tapeworm, and toxoplasmosis.
>
> If left alone with large quantities of food, a hog will literally eat itself to death. It has no stop button when it comes to eating. Swine are analogous to gluttons—in other words, the swine is to the animal world what the glutton is to humanity. Swine are one of the creatures that God apparently intended to be cleansers of the toxins of the earth. What they consume is to a great extent what we should not consume![34]

The Bible is right; pigs are not food. Pigs are scavengers, designed by God to keep the earth clean. They eat our refuse, and then we turn around and eat them?

A few years ago I was studying the Bible with a man, and the subject of clean and unclean foods came up. I explained to him in some detail why the pig is considered unclean.

"You don't have to convince me!" he exclaimed. "I quit eating pork years ago."

I was curious. "Do you mind if I ask why?" (If you have got a weak stomach, this might be a good time to skip to the next chapter.)

He straightened up in his chair. "Years ago in Europe, I was at a friend's house for dinner and I asked if I could use the restroom. He told me they didn't have one inside; they still had an outhouse.

"I went outside, and when I opened the outhouse door I suddenly heard a terrible racket coming from deep inside. There was a tunnel from the pigpen to the shaft of the outhouse, and every time the pigs heard the door open they came running, because they wanted to eat whatever was about to come down!

"I went back inside the house as they were serving roast pork. I couldn't eat it then, and I haven't touched in since."

His disgusting tale confirmed what I already know from the pages of the Bible. Pork is not food. Pork is nature's garage pail. It is riddled with toxins, and eating it helps speed you along to your grave.

We were never meant to eat scavengers. That also includes the scavengers of the sea:

"These you may eat of all that are in the water: whatever in the water has fins and scales, whether in the seas or in the rivers—that you may eat...Whatever in the water does not have fins or scales—that shall be an abomination to you." (Leviticus 11:9, 12)

As it did with land animals, the Bible gives us a safe rule for eating seafood. If it has both fins and scales, it's safe to eat. The list of clean seafood is quite long and includes salmon, trout, walleye, tuna,[35] halibut and cod. These fish are safe to eat, although it should be remembered that in recent years the level of toxins in our waters has made some clean fish unfit for human consumption as well.

Fish that do not have fins and scales are unclean. This list includes catfish, eel, squid, octopus, shrimp, lobster, shellfish, and many others. This was a particularly disappointing discovery for me, because I had always enjoyed some of these things. It didn't take much research, however, to convince me to give them up.

For the most part, unclean fish are the garbage pails of the sea. Many of them are filter-feeders, which means that they obtain their food by filtering the surrounding water through their bodies. They retain the nutrients found in that water—*and* the toxins.

There was a puzzling outbreak of severe gastroenteritis, sometimes referred to as "stomach flu," in Louisiana some years ago that baffled experts in disease control. They had trouble figuring out what had caused it, until their research led them to oyster beds:

Polluted water can easily transmit disease by contaminating shellfish. Just how easily was demonstrated in November 1993, when cases of foodborne disease began popping up in Louisiana. Eventually fifteen separate groups of individuals in Mississippi, Maryland and North Carolina would be made ill—127 people all told. The outbreaks were associated with eating raw oysters. Norwalk virus, an emerging pathogen, was identified as the agent in stool analysis. While there is no such thing as "stomach flu," influenza being a respiratory disease accompanied by fever and body aches, there are foodborne diseases caused by viruses—most often transmitted by food and water, just like bacterial pathogens. Viral causes are often missed in diagnosing foodborne disease because most laboratories don't routinely test for viruses.

Oyster beds are incredibly sensitive to what happens around them. In the 1993 case the implicated oysters were traced to two adjacent beds. The first thought was that they had been contaminated with raw sewage, but the nearest sewage outlet was sixteen kilometers away and fecal counts at the site were not particularly high. The investigators then turned to the local fishermen. They interviewed workers on forty boats at three docks and on twenty-six boats fishing in the sea. On twenty-two of the boats they discovered that either the toilets flushed directly into the sea or buckets were used and the contents tossed overboard. Two of the fishermen had been ill with gastroenteritis, and both tested positive for antibody titers to Norwalk virus. Each reported defecating and vomiting into a bucket that was then dumped overboard.

The investigators would later estimate that in a case like this where the infected material was dumped directly into the sea, one infected person could contaminate an area 100 meters [328 feet] wide and 1 kilometer [3,200 feet] long. That was about half the size of the area being harvested. The oysters consumed the virus along with plankton, but it accumulated and remained in their bodies for some time. Tests in the laboratory indicated that the virus could be present in the oyster for as long as twenty-five days and recent unpublished studies seem to indicate that the virus can survive cooking—very bad news indeed.[36]

Shellfish were designed by God to purge the oceans of filth, not for human consumption. Let's ask some probing questions about our practice of eating them. Why is it that we are willing to eat something that is served whole, including the intestinal tract? Why is it that sewage outlets are great places to catch shrimp? Just what *is* that dark line down the middle of the shrimp's body?

I remember hearing about a man a few years ago that tragically never resurfaced after scuba diving near my home. A team of divers hunted for his body, but they were unable to find him—until someone noticed a large pile of shrimp feeding on something on the ocean floor. When they brushed some of them aside, they found the body. Had they not found the body, the shrimp would have completely consumed it, because they're scavengers. God never intended for us to eat shellfish. They are toxic. There is a reason so many people die every year from eating bad shellfish.

Now let's look at birds. The eleventh chapter of Leviticus names a long list of unclean birds, such as vultures, crows and owls. Unfortunately, no simple distinguishing physical characteristics are given, but a few common sense principles will help you discern. The unclean birds are either scavengers or birds of prey. The clean birds—chicken, turkey, pheasant, quail and so on —all seem to have a crop and a gizzard.

We don't need to spend a lot of time making distinctions between clean and unclean birds, because we are not in the habit of eating unclean birds in North America. Most of the birds available in the supermarket are clean.[37]

The Bible's list of clean and unclean animals makes perfect sense. It is not a good idea to consume scavengers after they have consumed our filth. You'll live longer if you don't!

What about Peter's vision?

There is a passage in the tenth chapter of the book of Acts we should examine carefully because it seems to be a source of genuine confusion for many people:

The next day, as they went on their journey and drew near the city, Peter went up on the housetop to pray, about the sixth hour. Then he became very hungry and wanted to eat; but while they made ready, he fell into a trance and saw heaven opened and an object like a great sheet bound at the four corners, descending to him and let down to the earth. In it were all kinds of four-footed animals of the earth, wild beasts, creeping things, and birds of the air. And a voice came to him, "Rise, Peter; kill and eat." But Peter said, "Not so, Lord! For I have never eaten anything common or unclean." And a voice spoke to him again the second time, "What God has cleansed you must not call common." This was done three times. And the object was taken up into heaven again. (Acts 10:9-16)

Any time the subject of clean and unclean foods is discussed, someone is bound to reference this story. With some show of triumph, they typically point out that God gave Peter permission to eat unclean meat. He didn't. That is not the point of the story at all. Look at the next verse carefully:

*Now while Peter **wondered** within himself what this vision which he had seen meant, behold, the men who had been sent from Cornelius had made inquiry for Simon's house, and stood before the gate. (Acts 10:17, emphasis added).*

This story has nothing to do with clean and unclean meats. The Bible tells us, first of all, that Peter wondered about the meaning of the vision. He knew that it couldn't possibly mean that pork chops, which were once unhealthy, were now suddenly good for you.

As Peter was pondering the meaning of the vision, a party of Gentiles suddenly showed up at his door. The first verses of this same chapter tell us that they had been sent by God to see Peter.

However, the presence of Gentiles presented something of a problem to a Jew. In Peter's day the Jews despised Gentiles as unclean. They compared them to dogs. They refused to go into their homes or eat with them.

This prevailing Jewish prejudice presented a tremendous obstacle to the spreading of the gospel to the world. How were the Gentiles supposed to receive the good news about Christ when the new Jewish Christians would have nothing to do with them?

God gave Peter the vision of the unclean animals to correct his prejudice. Read the story carefully in it's context, and you'll see what I mean. When Peter wakes up, Gentiles who need to hear the gospel are knocking at his door. Suddenly, Peter understands what God was trying to tell him:

*Then he said to them, "You know how unlawful it is for a Jewish man to keep company with or go to one of another nation. But God has shown me that I should not call any **man** common or unclean." (Acts 10:28, emphasis added).*

Then Peter opened his mouth and said: "In truth I perceive that God shows no partiality." (Acts 10:34)

We must never ignore biblical context. This vision has nothing to do with pigs and has everything to do with people. Its message is clear: we are not to consider any person as unworthy of the gospel message.

Does God's prohibition against unclean meat still apply? Absolutely. In addition to Acts 10, there are a couple of other texts that have sometimes caused some confusion over the Bible's counsel on diet. The first one we will examine is found in Mark's gospel:

So He said to them, "Are you thus without understanding also? Do you not perceive that whatever enters a man from outside cannot defile him, because it does not enter his heart but his stomach, and is eliminated, thus purifying all foods?" And He said, "What comes out of a man, that defiles a man." (Mark 7:18-20)

Some have taken this passage to mean that Jesus declared all of the unclean foods to be clean.[38] If this were true, however, why did Peter years later protest in horror at the thought of eating unclean meat?

And a voice came to him, "Rise, Peter; kill and eat." But Peter said, "Not so, Lord! For I have never eaten anything common or unclean." (Acts 10:13, 14)

Remember that Peter doubted the meaning of the vision. He knew it couldn't possibly mean that unclean meats were now clean, and that's because he knew nothing of a command of Jesus that made unclean animals fit to eat.

What does the passage in Mark 7 mean then? Again, context is everything. Notice that the chapter begins with a controversy over ritual cleansing (not over pork chops):

"'And in vain they worship Me, Teaching as doctrines the commandments of men.' For laying aside the commandment of God, you hold the tradition of men—the washing of pitchers and cups, and many other such things you do." He said to them, "All too well you reject the commandment of God, that you may keep your tradition." (Mark 7:7-9)

The prohibition against eating unclean animals is hardly a "commandment of men" or a tradition. It is firmly rooted in the Word of God. This chapter in Mark is referring not to the clear dietary regulations of the Bible, but rather to the ceremonial washing rituals the Pharisees forced on people. The food in question was not meat, but bread:

Now when they saw some of His disciples eat bread with defiled, that is, with unwashed hands, they found fault. For the Pharisees and all the Jews do not eat unless they wash their hands in a special way, holding the tradition of the elders. When they come from the marketplace, they do not eat unless they wash. And there are many other things which they have received and hold, like the washing of cups, pitchers, copper vessels, and couches. Then the Pharisees and scribes asked Him, "Why do Your disciples not walk according to the tradition of the elders, but eat bread with unwashed hands?" (Mark 7:2-5)

When the disciples neglected to wash their hands, the bread they ate was considered unclean by tradition, and in turn, the disciples themselves were considered unclean.

In this story Jesus points out the error of the Pharisees. It is not outward acts that make our hearts pure or impure; it is our motives. The

Pharisees, in spite of their outward conformity to religious procedure, were less spiritually healthy than those whose motives were right but whose outward conformity to ritual was not perfect. Jesus' lesson is more about the heart than the stomach:

"For from within, out of the heart of men, proceed evil thoughts, adulteries, fornications, murders, thefts, covetousness, wickedness, deceit, lewdness, an evil eye, blasphemy, pride, foolishness. All these evil things come from within and defile a man." (Mark 7:21-23)

This is the whole point of the passage. Bread, says Jesus, simply passes through your system and disappears—whether or not you washed your hands. You are not unclean because you forgot a human tradition. You *are* unclean, however, if you cherish sin, because it is the heart that makes a person unclean, not the stomach. This passage has nothing to do with whether or not pork is clean; it has everything to do, however, with whether or not a person's heart is clean.

One last passage that sometimes causes confusion is found in Paul's first letter to Timothy:

Now the Spirit expressly says that in latter times some will depart from the faith, giving heed to deceiving spirits and doctrines of demons, speaking lies in hypocrisy, having their own conscience seared with a hot iron, forbidding to marry, and commanding to abstain from foods ["meats" in the KJV] which God created to be received with thanksgiving by those who believe and know the truth. For every creature of God is good, and nothing is to be refused if it is received with thanksgiving; (1 Timothy 4:1-4)

Some have taken this text to refer to those who recognize, live by, and teach the Bible's health principles. A careful reading, however, precludes this understanding. You'll notice that this passage is referring to "meats" (the old KJV word for "food") that God created to be received with thanksgiving. The Bible is clear that God did not create pigs to be received with thanksgiving.

The next verse throws a little more light on the subject: "...for it is sanctified by the word of God and prayer" (1 Timothy 4:5).

The word of God does not sanctify pigs; however it does sanctify cows. It's as simple as Paul referring to people who force arbitrary regulations on others apart from what has been prescribed by God Himself. This passage is not a license to eat unclean animals. What God declared to be unhealthy thousands of years ago is still unhealthy.

It might be stressed again at this point that many Christians are, in addition to avoiding unclean meats, choosing to avoid all flesh foods altogether. Given the conditions associated with mass production of animals for slaughter, the hormones and antibiotics livestock are subjected to, and the emergence of serious life-threatening contaminants and diseases, many are turning back to God's original vegetarian diet and finding that they enjoy life more when they feed their bodies the best nourishment. It's not mandatory, but it's certainly recommended!

In case some are still tempted to think that God's prohibition against unclean foods was only for the Jews, it might be worthwhile to study a passage in the book of Isaiah that makes it abundantly clear that it still applies to modern-day Christians. While talking about the Second Coming of Jesus Christ, an event that takes place long after the cross, Isaiah mentions something very interesting:

For behold, the LORD will come with fire and with His chariots, like a whirlwind, to render His anger with fury, and His rebuke with flames of fire. For by fire and by His sword the LORD will judge all flesh; and the slain of the LORD shall be many. "Those who sanctify themselves and purify themselves, to go to the gardens after an idol in the midst, eating swine's flesh and the abomination and the mouse, shall be consumed together," says the LORD. (Isaiah 66:15-17)

The language of this verse makes it clear that the events it describes take place at the Second Coming, after centuries of Christianity. The distinction between clean and unclean food still applies at that time. Those who knowingly consume unclean foods against God's will have indicated to the courts of heaven that they do not believe or trust Him.

In the new earth, as in Eden at the beginning, Scripture records that there will be no destruction of life. "They shall not hurt nor destroy in all My holy mountain, says the Lord" (Isaiah 65:25). Those who have the privilege of living there will once more subsist on the products of the earth. Ezekiel writes:

Along the bank of the river, on this side and that, will grow all kinds of trees used for food...Their fruit will be for food, and their leaves for medicine." (Ezekiel. 47:12)

John the Revelator saw the same vision of the heavenly home where sin would be banished, death abolished, Eden restored, and God's law of love exemplified in every detail: moral, universal and natural (Revelation 21-22).

Just as there was no sin and no death in the beginning in Eden, so it will be in Eden restored—the new earth. Life on this earth today is a preparation for eternal life in the earth made new. Thus it seems logical that the people of God today would choose, in every possible respect, to live a lifestyle here that emulates the lifestyle which will be experienced in the new earth, including a diet similar to that of Eden: the vegetarian diet.

Throughout the history of this world there have been those who chose, even at great risk (as illustrated in the story of Daniel and his friends—Daniel 1) to eat a diet in harmony with that originally provided by God to Adam and Eve in Eden. The same diet will again be followed in Eden restored.

We are living in the final days of this earth's history. Christ looked prophetically down the stretches of time and saw the world awash with moral pollution of every kind. To protect us from these delusions by keeping our minds clear and sharp, God in His infinite wisdom and love gave His remnant people a scientifically vindicated message of healthful living. Given in a language all can understand, this message describes a lifestyle that, above and beyond its many health benefits, preserves moral integrity.

The apostle John expressed his great longing when he wrote:

Beloved, I pray that you may prosper in all things and be in health, just as your soul prospers. (3 John 2)

In essence, I believe the Bible's teaching on health boils down to God pleading with us for our cooperation. It's as if He is saying, "I hate death and I hate disease. I want to give you every fighting chance possible to live a full and happy life. I have a lot invested in you. It cost Me everything to redeem you. So take care of what you've got, and you'll be better off all around." Here is Paul's entreaty:

I beseech you therefore, brethren, by the mercies of God, that you present your bodies a living sacrifice, holy, acceptable to God, which is your reasonable service. (Romans 12:1)

---

[21] Admittedly, E. coli and other contaminants are making their way into our plant foods as well, often thanks to careless cross-contamination.

[22] The first record of such permission, at least, is found in Genesis 9:3, 4.

[23] Does this mean that a vegetarian diet is mandatory for Christians? Probably not as the consumption of flesh foods was common throughout most of Scripture. Most Bible scholars accept that Jesus Himself was probably not a vegetarian during his earthly ministry, although that point is argued by some (see Luke 24:42-43). Read on, as there are plenty of other excellent reasons to choose be a vegetarian.

[24] According to traditional biblical chronology.

[25] Adventist Health Study-1.

[26] Archives of Internal Medicine, June 11, 2001; 161:1381-1389.

[27] Ibid.

[28] Laird S. Goldsborough, "Must Our Pork Remain Unsafe?" *Reader's Digest,* March 1950.

[29] *Facts About Trichinosis,* USDA APHIS Veterinary Services, APHISW 91-4, May 1972.

[30] Don Colbert, M.D., *What Would Jesus Eat?* (Nashville: Thomas Nelson, 2002), pp. 49, 50.

[31] *Facts about Trichinosis.*

[32] http://www.cdc.gov/ncidod/dpd/parasites/trichinosis/factsht_trichinosis.htm#common

[33] www.fsis.usda.gov/Is_It_Done_Yet/Brochure_Text/index.asp

[34] Don Colbert, *What Would Jesus Eat?* (Nashville: Thomas Nelson, 2002), p. 49.

[35] Some question whether or not tuna has scales. I have checked with reliable sources. It does have scales, although they are quite fine.

[36] Nicols Fox, *Spoiled* (New York: Basicbooks, 1997), p. 53.

[37] One exception is the ostrich, which is growing in popularity but is unclean.

[38] Some modern translations have actually mistakenly translated it this way.

CHAPTER FIVE

Tobacco

The Silent Killer[39]

An unbelieving world watched in horror as two commercial passenger jets smashed into the World Trade Center, one after the other. All possible routes of escape were cut off for those who worked above the points of impact, because the building was hopelessly engulfed in flames. Thick, black, toxic smoke made it impossible for a helicopter to pick survivors from the roof. There was no way out; they were destined to die. We watched in disbelief as some chose to leap to their deaths rather than wait for the flames to do the job.

Understandably, the enraged nations of the West immediately sprang into action. They denounced the terrorists as cowards and vowed to track them down. Armies were deployed to Afghanistan, and no expense was spared in trying to bring Osama bin Laden to justice. Nobody wants someone like that on the loose.

As heinous as that crime was, however, the Al Qaeda terrorist network was not the biggest killer in New York City that year. Someone else knowingly killed more than 10 times as many people; yet, to a large extent, we have failed to register our indignation.

When Christopher Columbus arrived in Central American back in the 15TH Century, the locals presented him with a pile of dried leaves. It was an unusual gift, and it left Columbus feeling a little awkward and confused. What should he do with them? His crew observed that the locals would light the leaves on fire and inhale the smoke. They tried it, and before their return to Europe most of them had become addicted to tobacco.[40]

In spite of Columbus, smoking didn't really catch on in Europe until Jean Nicot, a French diplomat, introduced it to France in 1556. (If his name seems vaguely familiar, it's because "nicotine" was named after him.) The French loved smoking, and with their endorsement it quickly spread to the rest of Western Europe. Today it is a worldwide bad habit.

By the early 1900s, cigarettes were being mass-produced and millions of people were smoking them with abandon. Oblivious to the lethal dangers lurking in the "weed," some actually believed it was good for them! Back in the mid 1800s, for example, doctors were known to prescribe smoking as a cure for lung ailments. One 1835 medical book recommended that while smoking "...the patient should frequently draw in the breath freely, so that the internal surface of the air vessels may be exposed to the action of the vapour."[41] In the 1900s, tobacco was prescribed to the general public for a rather amazing array of other ailments:

Tobacco had also been considered a treatment for migraines, a balm for stress, a mental stimulant, an efficient laxative, a remedy for toothache, worms, lockjaw, halitosis—even cancer.[42]

Nicotine became the drug of choice for millions. Statesmen, movie stars, and all the "who's who" used it. Anybody who was somebody smoked. In the mid-1900s, however, the tide was turned as shocking new information came to light. It turned out cigarettes were not a good idea at all. In fact, they were lethal.

During the years leading up to the 1950s, researchers discovered that cigarettes deliver more than just a dose of nicotine and a little bit of tar. They also dispense a considerable number of other carcinogens, and there was a demonstrable link between smoking and diseases like lung cancer and heart disease.

Obviously, when this information hit the newsstands, smoking suddenly lost a lot of its sheen. A now-famous 1952 article in *Reader's*

Digest, "Cancer by the Carton," made the news widely available, and the tobacco industry suffered its first decline in sales in more than 20 years.

Modern research dramatically confirms what *Reader's Digest* told the public back in the 1950s. Cigarette smoke is composed of 4,000 chemical compounds, more than 40 of which have been proven to be carcinogenic, including such notorious assassins as benzene, cadmium, chromium, radon and vinyl chloride.[43] In addition to these carcinogens, tobacco smoke is also known to harbor arsenic, acetone, formaldehyde, mercury, lead and even hydrogen cyanide. It's a lethal cocktail!

The tobacco companies were not content to sit idly by while their fortunes dwindled, and in 1954 they struck back, forming the Tobacco Industry Research Council to address the public's new fear of cigarettes. The Council hit upon a solution—a new breed of "safer" or so-called "healthier" tobacco products, including filtered cigarettes and low-tar cigarettes.

It worked. Tobacco sales bounced back as the public quickly forgot their fears. Cigarette consumption continued to net the industry billions of dollars in sales. The victory was destined to be short-lived, however, since the truth about tobacco could not be concealed forever.

In 1964 Dr. Luther Terry, the Surgeon General of the United States Public Health Service, released a widely publicized study which proved that cigarette smoking causes both lung and larynx cancer. In the words of his report, "cigarette smoking is a health hazard of sufficient importance in the united States to warrant appropriate remedial action."[44]

The news was considered so earth-shattering that is was deliberately released on a Saturday morning to avoid sending the stock market into a tailspin.[45]

The tobacco giants refused to give up, and for years the industry tried to cover up the facts about cigarettes. Publicly, they denied that cigarettes were either harmful or addictive. Privately, they knew it was true.

In 1988, during a lawsuit aimed at the tobacco industry, investigators discovered a confidential document prepared by the Philip Morris Tobacco Company that referred to cigarettes as "a dispenser for a dose of nicotine."[46] Using that kind of language, it was difficult for Philip

Morris to argue any longer that cigarettes were not highly addictive. Investigators also turned up other evidence that tobacco companies were deliberately targeting young teenagers as "replacement customers" for those who had already been killed by smoking.[47] The cover-up was shattered.

Even though they had been caught red-handed in their suppression of the truth, it still took more than 10 years for Philip Morris to admit what the investigators had uncovered. In 1999, 35 years after the Surgeon General's 1964 warning, the world's largest tobacco company finally admitted publicly on its website that tobacco smoking is both addictive and causes lung cancer, emphysema and heart disease.

It was over. Tobacco lost its case. Cigarette packages now have mandatory warning labels on them, many of which are graphic. Today, minors are forbidden to buy cigarettes. There are tight controls on advertising tobacco products. It is illegal to label cigarettes as "mild" or "light," because it gives consumers the false impression that some cigarettes aren't harmful.

You would think that the mountain of scientific evidence proving tobacco to be a killer would squash our desire to smoke; but people are still smoking. In fact, *lots* of people! Approximately one-quarter of the North American population still smokes cigarettes.[48]

So what? It doesn't hurt anybody but the smokers, right? Think again.

The tobacco habit is costing *all* of us more than we realize. For example, in 1992 Canadian taxpayers alone shelled out more that $2.6 billion in direct health care costs for tobacco-related disease.[49] When you add in all of the related costs, such as law enforcement and lost productivity, the bill swells to almost $9.4 billion a year.

That is an enormous sum of money, even by modern standards. When you take into consideration all of the federal and state or provincial programs that constantly lack for funding, and the shortfalls in the health-care budget, it becomes nearly impossible to defend the notion that the tobacco habit doesn't hurt anyone but the smoker. We are *all* paying for it—and not just with our wallets.

As far back as 1974, the Ontario Medical Association identified a need to protect those who do not use tobacco products yet are still exposed to lethal secondhand smoke. Recent research confirms that people who live and work with smokers also get lung cancer. In fact, secondhand smoke ranks as the third most preventable cause of death in Canada.[50]

Incredibly, in the province of British Columbia alone, secondhand smoke causes more workplace deaths than the logging, trucking and construction industries combined. For the 10-year period ending in 1998, workplace deaths in the BC logging, trucking, and construction industries claimed 492 lives. By comparison, secondhand smoke in the workplace laid claim to an estimated more than 3,000 lives.[51] It shouldn't be that way.

Children are also paying for other people's bad habits. The Surgeon General of the United States reported in 1994 that children who live with smokers are far more likely to suffer ear infections, asthma and breathing problems.[52] Evidence is also mounting that there is a link between cigarette smoking and some cases of Sudden Infant Death Syndrome (SIDS).

The facts have been in for years. Tobacco is a killer and a thief. On a worldwide basis, more than 1.5 million middle-aged smokers die each year. On average, they die 22 years earlier than the normal life expectancy.[53] That's a lot of valuable time lost for no good reason. Think of the children and grandchildren who are cheated at their graduation or wedding because a family member has been lost to tobacco. Think of the person living out his or her retirement alone because a spouse couldn't or wouldn't quit.

The death toll that tobacco smoke has pushed on us is staggering. Some have estimated that tobacco killed more than 45,000 people in New York City during the same year as the terrorist attacks on the Twin Towers. Weigh that number carefully, because it represents more than 10 times as many people as the terrorists killed. Incredibly, instead of becoming outraged people still line up to buy cigarettes!

The young are particularly vulnerable. A disturbing trend has recently been observed in the use of tobacco among high school students in the United States. The Centers for Disease Control reports that during

1998 to 2003 tobacco use in this age group was stable or decreased significantly, but those gains were halted between 2003 and 2005.[54]

Twenty-eight percent of high school students continue to use tobacco products! Every day in the United States, approximately 4,000 young people between the ages of 12 and 17 years begin smoking cigarettes and an estimated 1,140 young people become daily cigarette smokers.[55]

Our young people are the field in which the tobacco industry finds its replacement smokers. For years they have been deliberate targets of advertising campaigns selling the lie that smoking enhances their lives. They will pay for that lie with their lives. Yet, much of the public continues to support the tobacco industry by buying their products, apparently oblivious to the fact that a portion of the money squandered on every pack of cigarettes will go straight back into a campaign to hook others.

Why do North Americans continue to smoke? Most people will tell you that they don't have a choice. They would love to quit, but they have been hopelessly addicted for years. To a degree, they're right; the addiction is powerful. Some studies indicate that nicotine may be as much as five times more addictive than cocaine or heroin. And yet, they're dead wrong; it is definitely not hopeless.

Because smoking robs us of the abundant life God intends for us to enjoy, He is willing to throw His weight behind our effort to quit. God is much bigger than any addiction, and He can give the smoker victory over his or her deadly habit. I have seen it happen hundreds, if not thousands, of times.

The Bible makes it clear—you cannot smoke and bring glory to God. Smoking is a sin. In fact, it is an act of vandalism, because our bodies belong to God.

Some people argue that they continue to smoke because they really enjoy it. As an ex-smoker myself, I frankly have trouble believing people who say this. Either they're not telling the truth, or they have a warped sense of enjoyment. When they look back over the thousands and thousands of cigarettes they have had (a pack-a-day smoker will go through 7,300 cigarettes a year), how many of those cigarettes really brought more joy to their lives? Not one! The only joy cigarettes bring is the relief of withdrawal pains. What kind of joy is that? They could have that kind of joy every day if they quit.

Others claim that they continue to smoke because it helps them deal with stress. Let's be honest; that simply doesn't make sense. Smokers endure far higher levels of stress than non-smokers. The toxic cocktail they absorb into their bloodstream with each cigarette causes a good deal of stress by forcing their body to work overtime to avoid an untimely death.[56]

Add to this physiological strain the growing scorn society is heaping upon smokers, the increasing difficulty of finding a place to smoke, constant bad breath, premature aging of the skin, and the escalating price of cigarettes, and you have got a formula for some real stress! Smoking does not alleviate stress. Smokers are merely trying to chemically assuage the stress that their chemical dependency causes in the first place. If they didn't smoke at all, they'd be much further ahead.

I have also heard it argued that smoking helps some people concentrate on mental tasks. Frankly, this is wishful thinking. Carbon monoxide and carcinogenic chemicals are not brain food. While nicotine does artificially excite certain parts of the brain, it also constricts the blood vessels that supply it.

As a result vital nutrients and oxygen aren't getting to your brain as they should, while many counterproductive compounds are.

There are much better ways to heighten mental alertness that do not endanger your life. Regular vigorous activity, pure water, and healthy dietary practices, for example, provide good quality oxygenated blood to the brain, clearing out the cobwebs without giving you a tumor!

Let's be honest. There are many *excuses,* but there are no good *reasons* to smoke. Nicotine is a lethal poison. It destroys the human machine. It is not God's will for you to smoke. Period.

If you wrestle with this lethal addiction, don't forget that God is in you corner, and He is willing to put all of heaven's resources at your disposal if you really want to quit. Lean on Him, and you will walk away from your cigarettes forever—even if you've failed a hundred times in the past. The Bible has a cure. I have seen it work for countless smokers.

Freedom from Tobacco—Today

You have tried to quit smoking, but with dismal results. Sometimes you last for a week or two, or even a couple of months, but you always end up crawling back. You're not proud of yourself, but you are hopelessly trapped. Right?

Wrong. You don't have to be a smoker. Honest. You still have the power of choice at your disposal. Go get a pen and piece of paper because you are going to want to take some notes. Jot the following Bible verses down and commit them to memory. Post them on your refrigerator. Better yet, find a non-smoking Christian to whom you can be accountable and go through these verses with them. Ready?

Okay. Today is going to be different than your previous attempts to quit. You're not going to struggle to quit; instead you're going to choose to accept victory over smoking as a free gift from God. There is a world of difference. Notice what Paul says:

But thanks be to God, who gives us the victory through our Lord Jesus Christ. (1 Corinthians 15:57)

Read that verse again, carefully. Does God make us struggle for victory? Does He make us earn it? Absolutely not! He gives it to us as a gift. You don't earn gifts. You don't struggle for them, either; you just accept them.

If someone anonymously left an envelope with your name on it in your mail box and it contained a thousand dollars, how hard would that be to accept? Not hard at all, right? You'd simply take it and keep it.

In faith, receive God's gift. There are no strings attached. Accept by faith that *at this moment God has turned you into a non-smoker.* It's done. You are not a recovering smoker—you are a *non*-smoker. It's as simple as that. Start living your life as a non-smoker, because now you *are* one. It feels good, doesn't it?

Why don't you pause for a moment, bow your head and thank God for what He has just given you.

As a new non-smoker, you need to remember what the Bible says:

Likewise you also, reckon yourselves to be dead indeed to sin, but alive to God in Christ Jesus our Lord. (Romans 6:11)

As a new non-smoker, you must recognize that smoking is sinful and "reckon yourself to be dead" to it. God has given you "non-smoking" as a gift. As far as smoking is concerned, you are *dead.*

Remind yourself of that the next time you walk into a convenience store and look at the cigarettes behind the counter. The devil is undoubtedly going to tell you that you are still a smoker. He will lie to you about the gift God has given you, and make you think you can't live without cigarettes. Don't believe it. Don't doubt God's gift. You *are* a non-smoker, dead to smoking because God says so.

Now that you have stopped smoking, your body is going to go through a period of detoxification. It will take a little time to flush all the junk out of your system. To speed up the process and make is more bearable, drink large amounts of water and eat lots of fresh fruit for the first four or five days. This will help flush the toxins out of your body.

Get outside every day, even if it's raining. Take long walks and breathe deeply. Your lungs and your brain will thank you for it!

Shower two or three times a day for the first week. Many of the toxins you have ingested are going to come out through the pores in your skin, and you will want to rinse them off. Try switching between hot and cold water several times, ending with cold to keep your blood pumping. Dry yourself vigorously with a towel. You'll be amazed how much it helps. (Not only will showering clean your skin and keep you blood moving, you'll also find that it's really hard to smoke in the shower.)

Remember, a craving's peak lasts only a few minutes. It might seem like an eternity, but it's really only 60 to 90 seconds. By God's grace, you can handle that. Breathe deeply a few times, remind yourself that you're dead to sin, and walk away. Dead people don't smoke.

There is one more passage in the Bible you should study carefully as you claim God's gift of victory:

But put on the Lord Jesus Christ, and make no provision for the flesh, to fulfill its lusts. (Romans 13:14)

What is Paul saying? Don't plan to fail. Get rid of all temptation. If God has given you the gift of victory over smoking, you don't need cigarettes, ashtrays or a lighter anymore. Get rid of them. Put them in a bag, drive to a dumpster far away from your house, and get rid of them. Put this book down and do it right now!

If you keep these items around you are announcing to heaven that you doubt God's promises and you are planning to fail. You haven't really believed or trusted Him. Non-smokers don't need cigarettes, ashtrays or lighters. Believe what God says and get rid of them right away—even the souvenir and the sentimental items.

Here is what you can expect to enjoy in the days to come, thanks to the fact that God has created your body with an amazing capacity to heal:

- In the next 20 minutes, your blood pressure and pulse rate are going to drop to a more normal level. The temperature of your feet and hands will increase to normal.
- After eight hours, your smoker's breath will disappear, the carbon monoxide level in your blood will drop to a normal level, and the oxygen will go back up to a normal level.
- After just one day, your chances of having a heart attack will decrease. After three days, you'll start breathing a little easier.
- After only three months, your blood circulation will improve, walking will become easier, and your lung function will increase by up to 30 percent.
- After one year, your risk of coronary heart disease is only half that of a smoker. After only two years, your risk of heart attack will be nearly the same as lifetime non-smokers.[57]

If you haven't done so already, find somebody to be accountable to and tell them what you've done, right away. Talk to your spouse, your doctor, your pastor, or somebody at church who will pray with you one to three times a day[58] for the next week or two, thanking God for your victory over smoking. You'll be amazed at the difference it will make to have somebody remind you several times each day how much God loves you and wants you to enjoy life more.

If you don't have somebody to talk to, try contacting the pastor of your local Seventh-day Adventist church. Many of them have helped people claim their victory over smoking in Jesus Christ. Some churches will even have a special smoking cessation program you can join.[59]

Tobacco consumption is a massive blight on human society. It ruins lives and wastes valuable resources. You can do something about the problem simply by refusing to be a part of it. Say "no" to the industry that routinely kills far more people than Osama bin Laden and all other terrorists. Stop making excuses and get the help you need. Start living the abundant life God has planned for you!

You can be sure that as you take this matter to God in prayer, He will respond. When I think about the remarkable lengths Jesus went to in order to secure your salvation, I know that He cares enough to help you get more out of life. The cross of Christ is by far the strongest argument for how much God is willing to do to help you. If He's willing to sacrifice His own Son to secure your salvation, how hard do you suppose a little smoking addiction is for Him to handle?

Now, enjoy a more abundant life—tobacco free.

———————————

[39] Much of this chapter is drawn from an It Is Written telecast by Shawn Boonstra that first aired in Canada in 2002.

[40] Most of this history of tobacco is based on material from Martin O'Malley, "Smoking Up a Storm," (CBC News Online: 2001, accessed April 2001): available from www.cbc.ca/news/indepth/smoking.

[41] Rene Noorbergen, *Ellen White: Prophet of Destiny,* (New Canaan, CT: Keats Publishing, 1972), p. 96.

[42] O'Malley, np.

[43] Physicians for a Smoke-free Canada, *Tobacco Smoke Components: Carcinogens,* March 1999.

[44] O'Malley, np.

[45] Ibid.

[46] Ibid.

[47] Ibid.

[48] Ibid.

[49] Physicians for a Smoke-Free Canada, *The Cost of Smoking,* July 1998

[50] *Ontario Medical Association position paper on second-hand smoke.* Available at www.oma.org; accessed January 2003.

[51] Airspace Action on Smoking and Health, *Deadly Fumes: British Columbia Workplace Death Tool Attributable to Secondhand Smoke 1989 to 1998,* August 2001, p. 10.

[52] Ibid.

[53] See statistics at www.stop-quit-smoking.com/quit-smoking-reason.html

[54] CDC. Tobacco Use, Access, and Exposure to Tobacco in Media Among Middle and High School Students—United States, 2004. MMWR 2006; 54 (12): 297-301.

[55] Substance Abuse and Mental Health Services Administration. (2005). Results from the 2005 National Survey on Drug Use and Health: (Office of Applied Studies, NSDUH Series H-27, DHHS Publication No. SMA 05–4061). Rockville, MD.

[56] Some studies indicate that the average 1.2 milligrams of nicotine present in a single cigarette is enough to kill you, seven times over, if it were injected straight into your bloodstream.

[57] This information comes from the American Cancer Society as found at www.stop-quit-smoking.como/qit-smoking-reason.html; accessed January 2003.

[58] A good schedule for prayer would be: first thing in the morning, on your lunch break, and in the evening after supper.

[59] The Breathe-free Plan to Stop Smoking has been conducted in thousands of Seventh-day Adventist churches around the world since 1962. A local Seventh-day Adventist Church can give you information about when the next plan will be held. Other organizations that provide programs for smoking cessation and helpful materials include the American Lung Association, the American Cancer Society and the American Heart Association.

CHAPTER SIX

Alcohol

Wounds Without A Cause

"Did you hear? Tim[60] had to drop out of school because he drank too much."

We all shook our head in amazement. Some of us laughed. That figures. That guy parties so much he has to take the weekends off! He drinks like a fish."[61]

When you're eighteen and without Jesus Christ, a small part of you admires a guy who can "hold his liquor:" that is, until his life comes to a screeching halt. When he's asked to leave an institution of higher learning because of a drinking problem, suddenly nobody admires him anymore. Instead, he joins the ranks of such notables as the guy who ran around the campus naked after a pub brawl and the freshman who got so drunk he threw his bed off the third-floor dormitory balcony.

Of course, the real tragedy is that many of the "Tims" of our world used to be honor students who bartered potentially bright futures for a bottle. Some even manage to acquire a criminal record or an unwanted child because of something stupid they did while drunk. That's quite a price to pay for a few laughs on a Saturday night, wouldn't you say?

In spite of the shameful price alcohol often charges its victims, I have met lots of people—including some well-meaning Christians—

who continue to defend alcohol consumption as a legitimate form of recreation. "There's nothing wrong with drinking," they say, sometimes rather heatedly, "as long as you do it in *moderation!*"

I've heard the "moderation" argument a thousand times. In fact, there was a time when I used it myself to defend social drinking. There is only one problem with it—it's completely unbiblical. Let me show you what the Bible actually says:

Wine is a mocker, Strong drink is a brawler, and whoever is led astray by it is not wise. (Proverbs 20:1)

You may notice that the Bible doesn't mention anything about "moderation" in this passage. It doesn't refer to "too much wine," or "too much strong drink." It simply warns us that there is no wisdom in alcohol consumption—end of story.

This verse has proven itself true millions of times throughout human history. The human cost associated with alcohol consumption is disproportionately high compared to any actual benefit we might imagine we receive from drinking.

In Canada[62] alone, alcohol consumption costs taxpayers more than $7.5 billion every year. As much as $1.3 billion of that amount is taken directly out of a public health care system that continually wants for funding.[63] More than 18 Canadians a day are killed by alcohol; and another 125 are seriously injured.[64] More than 86,000 people are hospitalized every year because of alcohol and spend more than one million days there.[65] In addition to accidental injuries, alcohol consumption has been linked to liver damage, brain damage, stomach cancer, heart disease, fetal deformities and dozens of other potentially lethal ailments.

A string of roadside corpses, broken families, battered spouses and neglected children bear worldwide testimony to the fact that the Bible is telling the truth: alcohol consumption is not wise. How many homes have been damaged by the bottle? How many violent domestic disputes were fueled by a trip to the liquor store? How many marriages end because of an indiscretion that occurred while under the influence of alcohol?

The toll alcohol exacts on our society is enormous. More than one-third of violent crimes committed are drenched in alcohol,[66] likely because of the fact that alcohol lowers our natural inhibitions and silences our conscience. Countless numbers of people are assaulted or murdered by those who would not have perpetrated the crime had they not been drinking. As the bottles empty, the prisons fill.

A major study by the Canadian Center on Substance Abuse states:

Police officers reported that 51 percent of arrestees were under the influence of a psychoactive substance at the time of arrest—53 percent of men and 44 percent of women. Alcohol was indicated much more often than illicit drugs: 33 percent of arrestees were considered under the influence of alcohol only, compared with 9 percent under the influence of illicit drugs only.

Alcohol intoxication predominated in violent crimes committed by the federal inmates. The following table shows the percentage of each crime associated with each type or combination of substance abuse:[67]

	Alcohol only	Illicit drugs only	Alcohol and drugs
Assualt	39%	9%	24%
Homicide	34%	7%	21%
Attempted Murder	30%	9%	24%

The price we pay for alcohol consumption is staggering. In the words of the great evangelist of yesteryear, Billy Sunday:

The salon is a liar. It promises good cheer and sends sorrow. It promises health and causes disease. It promises prosperity and sends adversity. It promises happiness and sends misery. Yes, it sends the husband home with a lie on his lip to his wife; and the boy home with a lie on his lips to his mother; and it causes the employee to lie to his employer. It degrades. It is God's worst enemy and the devil's best friend. It spares neither youth nor old age. It is waiting with a dirty blanket for the baby to crawl into the world. It lies in wait for the unborn.

It cocks the highwayman's pistol. It put the rope in the hands of the mob. It is the anarchist of the world and its dirty red flag is dyed with the blood of women and children. It sent a bullet through the body of Lincoln; it nerved the arm that set the bullets through Garfield and William McKinley. Yes, it is a murderer. Every plot that was ever hatched against the government and law, was born and bred, and crawled out of the grog-shop to damn this country.[68]

Nothing has changed since Billy Sunday preached those words last century. Alcohol still promises everything, but delivers worse than nothing. It destroys bright minds, steals food and clothing from innocent children, and fills courtrooms with stories of ruined lives. It lowers inhibitions and encourages our basest passions. It is a cruel thief smuggled into the world by the father of liars and chief of murderers (John 8:44).

The financial toll on the individual is also tragic. Every dollar spent on drinking is utterly wasted—gone forever—and what do you have to show for it the next morning? Nothing except an empty wallet, a hangover, some really embarrassing memories, and perhaps a criminal record or unwanted pregnancy.

I love the frank honesty of the Word of God:

Who has woe? Who has sorrow? Who has contentions? Who has complaints? Who has wounds without cause? Who has redness of eyes? Those who linger long at the wine, those who go in search of mixed wine. Do not look on the wine when it is red, when it sparkles in the cup, when it swirls around smoothly; (Proverbs 23:29-31)

It may have been written many centuries ago, but nothing much has changed, has it? Drunks still complain. They still "cry in their beer," pick frivolous fights, and have many of regrets. Every weekend, emergency rooms are full of people with unnecessary injuries—wounds without cause. Solomon continues:

At the last it bites like a serpent, and stings like a viper. Your eyes will see strange things, and your heart will utter perverse things. (Proverbs 23:32, 33)

According to the Bible, there is a good reason everybody in the bar looks attractive at two o'clock in the morning. Your judgment in skewed. To put it in the nightclub vernacular, it's because you've got your "beer goggles" on. You are having trouble weighing consequences, because your inhibitions have been chemically lowered. As a result you do and say things you wouldn't otherwise do or say. You feel free to use coarse language. You sleep with people you're not married to.

God's advice is simple; **stay away!** In the end, alcohol is going to bite like a serpent and sting like a viper. It will poison your body and mind, and leave you more pain than you care to deal with when you sober up. It will fill your life with woe:

Woe to men mighty at drinking wine, Woe to men valiant for mixing intoxicating drink…(Isaiah 5:22)

There is a good reason the Bible prohibits the consumption of alcohol. Let's be honest about it. Christians can't drink to the glory of God. Alcohol damages our God-given body (even one drink kills brain cells), foists economic and social hardships on those who must reside in the community with you, and makes it much easier for you to slip into sin. There is no such thing as a good reason for Christians to drink.

Then why did Jesus turn the water into wine?

That is a fair question. Did Jesus really turn water into wine? Yes and no. Yes, because the second chapter of John is clear that Jesus turned water into wine. No, because the wine Jesus created wasn't the wine we typically think of in 21ST Century North America.

In the Bible, both grape juice and alcoholic wine are simply referred to as "wine." One word is used to describe both the alcoholic and non-alcoholic versions of the same beverage. Take a good look at the passage from Proverbs 23 again and you will see that the Bible forbids wine that "swirls around smoothly" or "sparkles in the cup." This is a description of alcoholic wine.

When the Bible says that Jesus turned water into wine at Cana, there are two possibilities: the wine was either alcoholic or it was non-alcoholic. When you take into consideration the biblical prohibition against alcohol, and the fact that Jesus came to give us life "more abundantly," which one is more likely? Can you really picture Jesus coming to a party at your house and handing out beer and cigarettes? It's not likely, is it? Read the story carefully:

Jesus said to them, "Fill the waterpots with water." And they filled them up to the brim. And He said to them, "Draw some out now, and take it to the master of the feast." And they took it. When the master of the feast had tasted the water that was made wine, and did not know where it came from (but the servants who had drawn the water knew), the master of the feast called the bridegroom. And he said to him, "Every man at the beginning sets out the good wine, and when the guests have well drunk, then the inferior. You have kept the good wine until now!"
(John 2:7-10)

Some have argued that the wine was alcoholic, the worst wines being saved for the end because drunkards wouldn't know the difference. I am not convinced by this argument because of something the governor said at the end of the feast: "This is the best wine I've ever tasted!" If he had been consuming alcohol up to that point (wedding feasts were known to go on for a very long time in those days), do you suppose he would have been able to tell the difference? Not at all. When you're drunk enough, shaving cream starts to taste good!

The governor was sober enough to recognize quality non-alcoholic wine when he tasted it. He wasn't drunk. Common sense alone tells us that the Son of God wouldn't do something to add to the misery of a fallen world or help lower the moral inhibitions of those He came to heal. God knows that roughly one-third of people who begin drinking socially develop a problem. He has witnessed the miserable effects of alcohol on human beings for thousands of years. Why would He contribute to a sinful problem? The wine He provided at the wedding was non-alcoholic.

So what do we make of the recent studies that seem to indicate that a glass of red wine several times a week is good for reducing cholesterol and preventing heart disease? There might be some truth to it, but is it worth the risk? Amputating your arm will alleviate the itch of a mosquito bite, too—but there are far better ways to do it. It is now known that a beneficial ingredient in the wine is the compound resveratrol.[69] This is a product of the red grape, and not the alcohol. Similar benefits can be obtained from unfermented grape juice, along with the use of other nutrition and health interventions, without risking the heartache the Bible warns us against.

It is interesting to note that even those experts who recommend moderate alcohol use as a preventive never urge those who do not drink to begin the habit. We must not forget that the longest-lived group of people in the United States, Seventh-day Adventists, do not use alcohol.[70] Regular exercise, careful diet, and a healthy lifestyle provide more benefit than wine without the considerable risks associated with alcohol.

Longevity may not be the biggest issue for Christians. In a world filled with temptation and allurement, we need to have unclouded minds that function at their peak performance so that we can distinguish and chose between that which is right and wrong, between the good and the bad. Alcohol intoxication washes away natural inhibitions and self-control, leaving a person without the necessary tools to live a principled and virtuous life.

We don't need more grog; we need more of God. There won't be a liquor store in heaven. Why should Christians want it now?

---

[60] The name has been changed to conceal this individual's real identity.

[61] Of course, it never seems to occur to most people who use this expression that a fish would never willingly consume alcohol.

[62] Editor's Note by Fred Hardinge, DrPH, RD: Pastor Shawn Boonstra was living in Canada when he wrote this chapter for the first edition of this book. A number of the references cite Canadian data on this topic. These have not been changed because they closely represent all of North America.

[63] Figures based on 1992 data. Single et al., *The Costs of Substance Abuse in Canada: Highlights of a major study of the health, social and economic costs associated with the use of alcohol, tobacco and illicit drugs*, Canadian Center of Substance Abuse, 1996.

[64] Based on 6,701 Canadian deaths in 1992. Ibid.

[65] Ibid.

[66] Canadian Center on Substance Abuse, *Proportions of crimes associated with alcohol and other drugs in Canada,* April 2002.

[67] Ibid.

[68] William T. Ellis, *Billy Sunday: His Life and Message* (Belfast: Ambassador Publications, 2001), p. 102.

[69] For information on resveratrol see the online encyclopedia Wikepedia at: http://en.wikipedia.org/wiki/Resveratrol

[70] Adventist Health Study-1.

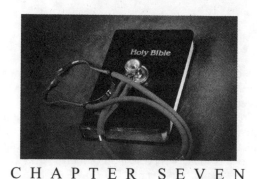

CHAPTER SEVEN

Caffeinated Beverages

Go-Go Juice

An Ethiopian goatherd was idly watching his herd while they nibbled on leaves and bright red berries. Before long they seemed to concentrate on just the berries. Soon after, they wandered out to the open pasture, and the goatherd noticed they were frisking about playfully. His young mind began to make a connection: red berries and extraordinary friskiness. He immediately walked over to the berry bushes and picked a handful of berries to eat himself. What a surprise; a sensation of pleasant elation overtook him. No wonder the goats were playful! And so, legend has it, coffee was discovered.

As a young man, I used to drink a lot of coffee. By the time I entered the university I was accustomed to drinking four pots of java every day: one with breakfast, one with lunch, one with supper, and a fourth one in the evening before I went to bed. That totaled something like twenty-four cups a day! Coffee is immensely popular. While not everyone drinks four pots a day, North Americans consume more than 400 million cups of their favorite drug every day.[71]

Why is it so popular? Ask any coffee drinker and they will tell you: "It gives me a great pickup. I can produce more work and be more effective. It helps me think better too." Like the Ethiopian goats, caffeine seemingly increases the speed at which animals perform learned tasks. Brain waves indicate arousal with increased voltage. Breathing is increased, blood pressure rises and reflexes become more responsive.

How does coffee do all these things when it has no real food value without the sugar and cream? How does it impart more energy? Actually, it really *doesn't* give any extra energy. Only food gives energy. However, the caffeine (trimethyl xanthine) in coffee facilitates the release of energy from body stores into the bloodstream, thus making it available for immediate use—at the expense of future needs. It's kind of like buying on credit. You don't have the necessary money, so you borrow it. Yes, you have the use of the items you purchased, but by the time the bills come due, the item may be already broken or useless.

It is the same way with caffeine-induced energy release. The payment date arrives several hours after one takes the drug, the result being increased fatigue, with *decreased* efficiency and alertness—and with interest due.

Many doctors are now telling their patients to kick the caffeine habit, and for good reason. Caffeine doesn't have one iota of nutritional value, and has been linked to sleep disorders, headaches, high blood pressure and tension, irregular heartbeat, memory loss, tremors and convulsions. Some studies suggest it also acts as a catalyst for carcinogens, increasing the odds of getting cancer.

According to Dr. Jan Kuzma, additional adverse side affects of caffeine consumption include unbalancing your autonomic nervous system, elevating your blood sugar and aggravating hypoglycemia. If that's not enough to make you consider giving it up, consider that caffeine consumption also increases urinary calcium and magnesium losses, which can lead to loss of bone density. It also constricts your blood vessels, increases stomach acid secretion (which can aggravate ulcers), causes tremors, increases anxiety and depression, and can heighten the symptoms of premenstrual syndrome. Just two cups of coffee a day will increase the risk of contracting fatal colon or bladder cancer.[72]

This may sound different than what you read in your local newspaper. Today there is a lot of conflicting information on the purported benefits or dangers of coffee use. Personally, I would rather not take the chance. Many of the pro-coffee studies I have seen also include advice for breaking the caffeine habit without suffering severe withdrawal symptoms. There's something wrong with that picture. I would rather not consume something that would cause withdrawal symptoms in the first place!

A careful reading of the literature will give you a more objective picture. Take, for instance, a research study published in the *American Journal of Clinical Nutrition* last year. This study looked at the effect of chronic caffeine consumption on the stiffness of the large arteries. When these arteries become stiff, the function of the heart and circulatory system is lessened. These researchers found that the chronic use of caffeine containing drinks had a significant detrimental effect that may raise the risk of cardiovascular disease.[73]

Dr. Kuzma mentions an interesting study done on typists:

> Researchers tested a group of typists who had used no caffeine for at least two weeks. Their typing was accurate and they correctly estimated their speed.
>
> In the second part of the test, each participant drank two cups of coffee. The typists' accuracy decreased considerably. However, in their self-evaluations they thought they were doing much better in speed and accuracy than when they had not used caffeine. The apparent improvement they felt in performance after imbibing caffeine was illusionary. This led researchers to say that although caffeine stimulates you when you are rested, it doesn't improve your performance beyond what you could accomplish with adequate rest and no caffeine.[74]

So much for the idea that caffeine improves your performance. On a construction site where I once worked, we used to call coffee "go-go juice," because everybody assumed that it improved our ability to get things done. It turns out that the only thing it improved was our self-estimate.

Popular thinking is that when we are too tired to carry on, a cup of coffee will keep us going. Think that concept through for a moment. There is something wrong with using a drug to make up for missing sleep. Our bodies get tired for a reason. Nature is trying to tell us to slow down and rest; yet we often force our system to keep performing with a good dose of coffee or cola, ignoring natural warning signs. How healthy is that?

When I'm driving at night, I sometimes wonder how many of the oncoming cars are being driven by someone forcing himself to stay awake with caffeine. People may think they are performing better with a dose of caffeine, but as Dr. Kuzma points out, this is an illusion; they only *think* they are performing better.

Common sense tells us that when we are tired we should go to bed. Sleep when it's time to sleep. Don't resort to poisoning your system.

"But you don't understand. I *have* to drive all night, and caffeine is healthier than a car accident!"

While that reasoning sounds very logical, it ignores the fact that our bodies build up a tolerance to caffeine. There are many cases of drivers trying to pull all-nighters who have had two or three cups of black coffee at a truck stop, have pulled back on the freeway, and promptly fallen asleep. There are far better ways to stay awake. Try drinking two or three quarts of water instead. I promise, when you've urgently got to use the bathroom you won't be able to fall asleep at the wheel!

Seriously, it would be better to give up the caffeine. You will find that you become more even-keeled, and are better able to cope with stress throughout the day. You will also sleep better and enjoy a more abundant life.

---

[71] http://www.e-importz.com/Support/specialty_coffee.htm
[72] Jan Kuzma, et al, *Live 10 Healthy Years Longer* (Nashville: Word Publishing, 2000), p. 67.
[73] Vlachopoulos, C, et al, Am J Clin Nutr 2005;81:1307–12.
[74] Ibid., p. 68.

C H A P T E R   E I G H T

Sleep and Fatigue

Don't Go Into Debt

I'll bet you think this chapter is about avoiding financial debt. Certainly staying out of debt will reduce your stress level and protect you from much unhappiness. Actually, we are going to look at another kind of debt you may never have thought about before.

While flying from coast to coast recently, I (Fred Hardinge) was engaged in a conversation with my seatmate about his successful business. He put great emphasis on how hard he worked and the long hours he kept. Then he made this startling statement: "I think sleep is the biggest waste of time—and I try to find employees who don't need any either!"

Unfortunately, we live in a society today that does not value the importance of rest and sleep. Like this businessman, sleep is considered to be a waste of time, and an option at best. This attitude has infected all age groups in our society. Over the past several decades, adults in the US have decreased the average number of hours of sleep by about 20 percent.[75] This means that we are sleeping 1.5 hours less than our grandparents. As a result, in 1999, 40 percent of Americans reported that they are so sleepy during the day that it interferes with their daily activities.[76] This also impacts our safety on the highways. The National

Transportation and Safety Administration reports that over 100,000 car crashes occur each year due to drowsy drivers.

Perhaps even more alarming is the dramatic decrease in the sleep time of teenagers. Seventy-five years ago this age group was sleeping eight to nine hours a night. Today however, that has dropped to seven hours or less,[77] even though teens actually need more sleep than when they were pre-teens. A nationwide survey[78] done in 1999 by the National Sleep Foundation found that 60 percent of teens under the age of 18 complain about being tired during the day, and 15 percent reported falling asleep at school.

Why is sleep necessary?

Depriving ourselves of sleep is much like depriving ourselves of food. If we eat fewer calories than we need each day, we will slowly lose weight because of a cumulative effect. When we deprive ourselves of sleep we accumulate a deficit of sleep over days in the same way. If you lose one hour of sleep each night over a week's time, at the end of the week you will have a sleep debt of seven hours, which is nearly the same as losing a whole night's sleep.

What is really surprising is that a sleep debt of three to eight hours will produce noticeable negative effects on your performance—physical and mental. Research on French cyclists who had lost only three hours of sleep, showed they fatigued faster than when fully rested.[79] Evidence continues to accumulate that relatively small amounts of sleep loss weakens the immune system and makes us more likely to succumb to infections and disease.[80]

Sleep debt also has a direct effect on thinking ability and mental efficiency. During the past 15 years, scores of studies have looked at this area with a very clear pattern of findings. Sleep debt produces a general slowing of most mental processes. Sleepy people have a very difficult time concentrating and keeping their attention fixed on the task at hand. Important information is frequently missed, and these lapses can be disastrous.

A momentary lapse while driving might result in not seeing a child running into the street, or an accountant may miss a number in a column of figures, thereby arriving at an incorrect conclusion. These momentary flickers in sustained attention are directly related to the amount of sleep debt.

Amazingly, research in Canada has shown that traffic accidents increase by eight percent in the 24 hours following the spring time-change when only an hour of sleep is usually lost, and an almost equal decrease in the fall when an hour is gained![81]

When we have to deal with a complex task with many parts, sleep debt can have a marked impact on our performance. A tired person may be able to recall information from their long-term memory with fair accuracy, but it is the short-term (immediate) memory that is most affected. This will have drastic effects on complicated tasks like important contract negotiations or driving a car on a busy freeway.

Even our moods are affected by sleep debt. Not only do tired people feel more fatigued and less vigorous, they also tend to become more depressed. As sleep debt increases, people lose their ability to enjoy things and activities they normally enjoy. They often withdraw from others as their irritability significantly increases.

The ability to exercise routine problem solving may remain intact with moderate amounts of sleep debt. However, novel and creative solutions to more difficult problems are much less likely to be forthcoming when we are tired.

As we become more tired we act more like an airplane on autopilot. We can usually handle the simple changes and the relatively ordinary demands of life, most of the time. However, anything out of the ordinary will increase the likelihood of our making significant errors. Motivation to tackle the tough tasks of life suffers also. Sleep deprived individuals are unwilling to work at tasks that require more than automatic performance.[82]

The bottom line is that when we allow ourselves to get tired our highest mental functions are compromised. When discernment, judgment, initiative and creativity are blunted we cannot make clear decisions. When decision-making is compromised, everything we do is negatively affected: our learning abilities, our reasoning abilities, our safety, our efficiency, our communication skills and our relationships.

Why do we build up sleep debt?

There are many reasons why so many of us do not get enough sleep. For most it is simply that we do not value sleep, and as humans we rarely choose to do that which we do not value. Some of the most common thieves of sleep are television, surfing the internet, entertainment, sports, overwork, stress and anxiety, night-shift work, noisy environments, the use of stimulants such a caffeine, many common medications and a sedentary lifestyle.

Ouch! That is a long and inclusive list, isn't it? While we love to blame the boss for making us work too much, we must honestly examine all our activities in light of our important priorities.

The spiritual impact of sleep loss

A pastor friend of mine was recently caught in immoral activity that cost him his job. As he looks back on that experience, he says that he allowed himself to become so tired and worn out that he could not resist the temptation to revert to behaviors he had engaged in before he became a Christian more than 25 years ago.

Fatigue probably has a more important impact on our spiritual lives than it has on our ordinary daily activities. Optimal decision-making capacity is necessary to differentiate between right and wrong. Yet when we are tired we have even less motivation and willpower to act on what we know is correct. Thus we fall into temptation more easily. Remember, for centuries sleep deprivation has been a most effective ingredient of brainwashing, and is even purposefully used today by professional labor and hostage negotiators.

For Christians, Bible study and prayer is our lifeline. The devil knows that if he can make us tired, even from being involved in the good activities of life, it will lessen our ability and interest in studying and understanding the Bible. It will also weaken our commitment to communicate with God in prayer.

How much sleep do we need?

Most sleep researchers agree that humans can "get by" on about seven hours of sleep each night. But how many of us want to just "get by" in life? The evidence is strong that for peak performance in all areas of our lives, we need between eight and nine hours of sleep each night. Our teenagers actually need 10 to 12 hours to maximize their learning and memory abilities, as well as to ensure proper growth and development. Obviously, getting those amounts of sleep requires careful choices and self-discipline.

Suggestions for staying rested

Here are a few things you can do to ensure you stay at your rested optimum:

• *Have a regular time for going to bed and a regular time to get up that allows you eight to nine hours of good sleep—and stick to your schedule.* Irregular schedules, especially for getting up in the morning, are like little doses of jet lag. We are creatures of habit. We maximize the value of our sleep when we have a regular plan for sleeping.

• *Exercise a minimum of 30 minutes each day, at least six hours before retiring.* Believe it or not, regular physical activity maximizes the value we get from our hours asleep.

• *Eat a healthful diet and avoid large, late, evening meals.* Large and late evening meals disturb our sleep patterns with prolonged digestive activity, and decrease the recuperative value of our sleep time.

• *Learn to control your stress and anxiety positively by putting your trust in God.* Guilt may be one of the greatest causes of insomnia. As Christians we can lay our burdens at the Cross and receive forgiveness from Christ. "When you lie down, you will not be afraid; Yes, you will lie down and your sleep will be sweet" (Proverbs 3:24).

• *Set aside one day each week for rest and recuperation and take a truly restful vacation each year.* The Sabbath, when properly observed, is a wonderful gift to the weary. The value of setting aside the frantic pace of life for twenty-four hours is inestimable!

• *Avoid the use of alcohol or stimulants and eliminate watching exciting or depressing television.* All of these things disturb the sleep patterns and detract from the rest we should be getting.

• *Sleep in a dark, quiet, cool room on a firm, comfortable bed.*

Following this advice will assure that you will get the greatest benefit from your time in bed.

• *When you are tired, take a 15 to 30 minute nap to restore rested performance.*[83] Taking a nap is the best first aid for tired people. It will temporarily restore performance to normal levels.

How Much Sleep Debt Do You Have?[84]

Here is a simple test you can take to estimate your sleep debt. Indicate the likelihood of your falling asleep in the following eight situations by placing the number corresponding to the scale in the table below.

Scale
> 0 = would never doze
> 1 = slight chance of dozing
> 2 = moderate chance of dozing
> 3 = high chance of dozing

Sleep Debt Test
> _____ 1. Sitting and reading
> _____ 2. Watching TV
> _____ 3. Sitting inactive in a public place (i.e., church, a meeting)
> _____ 4. As a passenger in a car for an hour without a break
> _____ 5. Lying down to rest when circumstances permit
> _____ 6. Sitting and talking to someone
> _____ 7. Sitting quietly after a lunch without alcohol
> _____ 8. In a car, while stopped for a few minutes in traffic

Total up each response to calculate your total score.

Your Score
> 5-5   = Slight or no sleep debt
> 6-10   = Moderate sleep debt
> 11-20 = Heavy sleep debt
> 21-24 = Extreme sleep debt

The FatigueBusters® Double Check Checklist[85]

❑ I feel tired.

❑ My sleep last night was shorter than 8 hours or of poor quality.

❑ I have been awake for more than 12 hours.

❑ During the past week I have slept less than 8 hours per night.

❑ Today I experienced unusual mental lapses and/or clumsiness.

❑ I am feeling irritable, upset or angry. Today has been
   especially stressful.

❑ I have recently been sick.

❑ I consumed alcohol or sleep-inducing medications during the
   past 24 hours.

❑ Today I drank less than 6-8 glasses of water.

❑ My meals were irregular today, or I had a large, fatty meal
   less than four hours ago.

How are you doing? If you checked one or more items, your decision-making ability, safety, emotions and communication skills may be seriously compromised.[86]

[75] Wake Up America: A National Sleep Alert, 1993.

[76] "Sleep In America" Survey, National Sleep Foundation, 1999.

[77] Wake Up America: A National Sleep Alert, 1993.

[78] http://www.sleepfoundation.org

[79] Mougin, et al., European Journal of Applied Physiology 63 (1991): 77-82.

[80] Sleep Research Online 1(4): 107-111, 1999.

[81] NEJM 334 (1996): 924.

[82] Engle-Friedman, et al, Sleep 22 (1999), 151.

[83] NASA Technical Memo 103884.

[84] This sleep assessment appears in William Dement's book, *The Promise of Sleep,* as well as having been published in other sources.

[85] © 1995 Total Life Creations. Fatigue Busters is a trademark of Total Life Creations.

[86] Fred Hardinge was the primary contributor to this chapter on sleep.

C H A P T E R   N I N E

Mental Health: Pure Thoughts

Guarding the Gates

When I first went into full time ministry there was absolutely no way I wanted a computer. I had a good electric typewriter, and as far as I was concerned that's all I needed. A high school graduation gift from my parents, it served me well throughout my university years, and was loyal to me through the first couple of years of my ministry. There was no good reason that it couldn't last the rest of my life.

Then I noticed that the ministers who owned computers seemed to get more done in less time. They didn't sit up half the night re-typing their sermons or have piles of crumpled paper on the floor behind their desks.

They didn't have to copy long passages of the Bible; they just clipped and pasted. And if they wanted to revise a sermon, all they had to do was type in the change and press a button to print another copy.

I caved in and begrudgingly bought a computer, bristling at what seemed like the exorbitant price. When I got it home and set it up, I found out why the "computer-savvy" guys got things done faster. It could file, sort, justify lines, clip, paste and store thousands of books and documents, all at the click of a mouse. It could even answer the phone for me when I was busy!

I was a convert. Who needs to grind away torturously at a typewriter when you can blaze along effortlessly at the speed of light on your computer? That first computer turned out to be one of the best investments I have ever made, a "rocket ship" that made my typewriter seem like a roller skate by comparison.

After a few months however, I learned something important about computers: the more you enhance them, the slower they run. When your computer is brand new, it almost never freezes up; but the more software you load on it, the more likely it is you'll run into problems.

It turns out that you're supposed to de-fragment the hard drive on a regular basis, because computers tend to store data wherever there's space on the drive, in little pockets scattered all over the place. Over time the hard drive becomes messy and slows down. I also learned (the hard way) that you can't indiscriminately install and uninstall dozens of programs on your computer and still expect carefree computing. Sometimes programs conflict with each other, resulting in almost daily freeze-ups.

Worst of all, I found out that you have to be exceptionally cautious about what sort of information you allow to be downloaded onto your computer from the Internet. An otherwise innocuous looking email message might be harboring a devastating computer virus, designed by some deviant who had nothing better to do than maliciously destroy other people's work.

Just as with your house, you need to put some form of security on your computer: virus-scanning software, passwords and firewalls. If you want to keep sensitive or private information safe in transit over the World Wide Web, you also need good encryption software. The hours of work you store in your computer—and the computer itself—are costly investments well worth protecting. Most of us make the effort to protect them.

Yet how many layers of protection do we put on the human mind? Your brain is a truly miraculous machine; it's capable of things your PC will never be able to do, such as imagining, sympathizing, dreaming, loving, reasoning and praying. The grey matter between your ears operates at lightning speed, processing something like 20 million-billion calculations per second (that's a two with 16 zeros behind it). It can multitask almost effortlessly. It regulates not only what you *know* but also who you *are*. If you lose your mind you lose everything. How many layers of protection have you placed on it?

When you feed conflicting information into your home computer, it will freeze up and give you an error message. What happens if you feed conflicting information into your mind? Would it also malfunction?

Absolutely. Not only is it a possibility, it is a reality for most of us. The Bible warns us of forces at work in this world that are deliberately trying to corrupt our minds, much like a hacker trying to break into a high-level government computer. Your mind, according to the apostle Paul, is the primary battleground for a great spiritual conflict:

For though we walk in the flesh, we do not war according to the flesh. For the weapons of our warfare are not carnal but mighty in God for pulling down strongholds, casting down arguments and every high thing that exalts itself against the knowledge of God, bringing every thought into captivity to the obedience of Christ...(2 Corinthians 10:3-5)

The Great Controversy between Christ and Satan is not being fought on a literal, geographical battlefield. It is rather being fought in the hearts and minds of human beings. Fallen angels are waiting for an opportunity to plant suggestions in your mind that would sever your line of communication with heaven, break down your moral inhibitions, and cause you to malfunction in your relationship with God.

As frightening as that may seem, we are not left defenseless. God has provided "virus protection software" for the human mind. You'll find it tucked away in the Bible passage you just read. Ask yourself: Is every thought captive to an obedient life in Christ? Is the information in your mind spiritually consistent? Does it harmonize with the Word of God? Does is reconcile with the mind of Christ?

If the answers to these questions are not "yes," you run the risk of a moral malfunction. Information inconsistent with Scripture has wormed its way into your thought processes. Over the long run, if you continue to download corrupted data it will make sin seem appealing, and may even cost you your eternal life. Perhaps that's why Paul gave the Philippian church this advice:

Finally, brethren, whatever things are true, whatever things are noble, whatever things are just, whatever things are pure, whatever things are lovely, whatever things are of good report, if there is any virtue and if there is anything praiseworthy—meditate on these things. (Philippians 4:8)

This is the Bible's virus-protection software for your mind. What you think is what you eventually become. Whether you develop a godly or worldly character has a lot to do with what you feed your mind. You simply cannot feed conflicting information into your mind forever and get away with it. Jesus said:

"No one can serve two masters; for either he will hate the one and love the other, or else he will be loyal to the one and despise the other. You cannot serve God and mammon." (Matthew 6:24)

When I was attending the university I didn't own a car, so when I wanted to take a girl on a date I had to take the bus or a taxi. It was an arrangement that dealt quite a blow to my young male ego. But I reasoned that a date in a taxi was better than no date at all!

One night I hired a taxi and picked up a nice young lady for a date. We went out for dinner at the best restaurant I could afford on a student budget, which wasn't much. When dinner was over, I called for another taxi and took her home.

After I dropped her off, the taxi driver asked me where I lived, assuming that I wanted to go home. I assured him that I had no such intention.

"Never mind where I live," I said. "I've got another date. Here's the address, and make it quick because we're running late!"

The driver looked at me in his rearview mirror and gave me a broad smile. "Hey kid," he said, with an air of father-knows-best, "take some advice. You're never going to get away with this. You can't go out with two girls at the same time!"

His unwelcome advice irritated me a little. "Let me worry about that," I retorted, and we were on our way.

We picked up my second date—another lovely young lady—and I went out for dinner a second time that night. After dinner I took her home. A few days later I learned an important life lesson: *Always* listen to your taxi driver! He was right; you can't go out with two girls at the same time and get away with it for long. My first date wondered why she was home before eight, and the second girl wondered why the taxi driver kept laughing to himself and winking at me the whole way to the restaurant. Both girls smelled a rat; and neither girl ever went out with me again.

You can't date two girls at the same time and get away with it. The Bible says you can't serve two masters, either. It will catch up with you. When it does, you will discover it was a very expensive mistake. If you dance at the devil's party, be certain that he's going to make you pay the cover charge.

Back in 1982 the ABC evening news ran a story about a strange work of art that had gone on display at a prominent gallery. It was a chair with a loaded shotgun attached and pointed to it. The gun was connected to a timer that was programmed to go off at random some time in the next 100 years. Visitors were invited to sit in the chair for one full minute and stare down the barrel of the gun, taking the chance that it might go off.

It's crazy, right? You would like to think that nobody is dumb enough to gamble with his or her life for no good reason. However, when the exhibit opened there was a line-up of thrill-seekers several blocks long.

Unfortunately, the same thrill-seeking tendency seems to be true of many Christians. After living through all the heartache and pain the devil has brought to our world, you'd think that no Christian would be willing or dumb enough to go and play in the devil's backyard; but there they are—splashing in his pool.

They brush aside the still small voice of the Holy Spirit. They gamble that the spiritual gun won't go off when it's their turn to sit in the chair, choosing to allow their minds to be pulled in two directions. This, in spite of the fact that the apostle James warns that a "double minded man is unstable in all his ways" (James 1:8).

In others words, if you load your mind with all sorts of conflicting information, it *will* become unstable. Count on it; it's a spiritual law. You simply can't have the world and still have Jesus. "Don't you know," warns James, "that friendship with the world is enmity with God?" (James 4:4) You have got to choose. Look at what the Bible says:

For whatever is born of God overcomes the world. And this is the victory that has overcome the world—our faith. (1 John 5:4)

The Christian born of God doesn't allow himself to play in the devil's yard. By faith he overcomes his sinful desire and cleanses his mind, because he realizes that you *are* what you *think*. Here is how Jesus described it:

"A good man out of the good treasure of his heart brings forth good things, and an evil man out of the evil treasure brings forth evil things." (Matthew 12:35)

According to Jesus, if you fill your mind with good things you will generate positive outcomes. Fill you mind with garbage, on the other hand, and you will generate misery. Your mind will start to spew evil thoughts like a backed-up sewer.

People often approach me complaining that they struggle with immoral or evil thoughts. More often than not this is the result of a poor diet for the mind. They have been providing it with the wrong things. In reply, one of the first questions I usually ask is: *"What are you feeding your mind?"*

Almost without exception, I discover that their prayer and devotional life is suffering or virtually non-existent. In other words, they haven't been supplying their minds with godly information. Furthermore, I usually discover that they have been doing just the opposite: nourishing their minds with garbage.

I remember a man who slid into the pew next to me one day and asked, "Pastor, it says in the Bible that even our thoughts need to be in obedience to Christ.[87] Is that true?"

"Yes," I said, "that's true."

"But Pastor!" he said with a good degree of exasperation in his voice, "how do you *do* that? How can you change the way you *think*? I can't control what pops into my mind. It makes me do things I don't really want to do. I can't control it!"

The fact is, things don't just "pop" into your mind any more than money just "pops" into your bank account. Either you have nourished your mind with evil thoughts yourself, or you have left the vault door wide open so others can dump their trash there.

In his book *The Holy War,* the famous Christian writer John Bunyan once compared the human mind to a city with five gates representing your five senses. The devil, he argued, continually storms the city of your mind by launching attacks against these five gates:

> This famous town of Mansoul had five gates, in at which to come, out at which to go; and these were made likewise answerable to the walls, to wit, impregnable, and such as could never be opened nor forced but by the will and leave of those within. The names of the gates were these: Ear-gate, Eye-gate, Mouth-gate, Nose-gate, and Feel-gate.[88]

John Bunyan hit the nail right on the head. The five senses are the five gates to your mind. Generally speaking, nobody can force the gates open; they can only enter with your permission. Except in rare situations, garbage does not make its way into your mind by accident. Typically, faulty information only makes it into your brain because you've lingered just long enough at the cesspool of filth to absorb its stench into your mind.

According to the Bible, all temptation boils down into three broad categories:

Do not love the world or the things in the world. If anyone loves the world, the love of the Father is not in him. For all that is in the world— the lust of the flesh, the lust of the eyes, and the pride of life—is not of the Father but is of the world. And the world is passing away, and the lust of it; but he who does the will of God abides forever. (1 John 2:15-17)

Almost every sin we are tempted to commit falls into one of these three categories: the lust of the flesh, the lust of the eyes, and the pride of life. The first category has to do with appetite, the second has to do with your senses, and the third has to do with the root of all sin: pride. If you play around in these three areas, you throw open the doors of your mind to fallen angels.

The whole point of temptation is to entice you to open the gate. Unless you open it, the devil cannot enter. He cannot read your mind.[89] He sits on the outside carefully studying you. He notes your wandering

however, how much of what the world listens to on the radio could be considered wisdom?

A few years back, following the example of another preacher, I took a notepad into my car and pushed the *scan* button on the radio. As best I could, I jotted down the lyrics to every song that came on. Most of it was raunchy enough that I have opted not to print the lyrics in a Christian publication. However, here is a synopsis of what I heard:

Song 1: A song demanding that people worship the singer, bow down to him, and serve him. Given the lifestyle (and life expectancy) of your average rock star, this could hardly be described as wisdom. Besides, the Bible is clear that only God is worthy of our worship.

Song 2: Honestly, as hard as I tried, I couldn't make out a single word of this song, in spite of the fact that it was supposedly in English. The "artist" was too busy screaming and shouting to bother with singing. I'm still not sure if he was involved in a song or torturing cats! The Bible states clearly in 1 Corinthians 14:33 that God is not the author of confusion, so I'm certain He was not the author of this song. Besides, if you can't make out what is being said, how much wisdom could there possibly be in it?

Song 3: No complaints here—it was Mozart's 33RD Symphony.

Song 4: A famous Phil Collins tune from the 1980s that describes a woman—an "easy lover"—who likes to take advantage of men sexually and then break their hearts. Few earthly fathers would want a man to sing this song about their daughters. I can't imagine that God enjoys hearing it either.

Song 5: This was a tremendously popular tune by Ricky Martin about living the "crazy life." There was simply too much here to comment on; however, the part about sleeping with a woman in a cheap motel and then being robbed by her after she drugged him left me convinced, beyond the shadow of a doubt, that choruses of heavenly angels probably weren't joining in with Ricky as he sang this song.

Song 6: This song repeatedly encouraged the listener to "bounce with me, bounce with me"—and they were not talking about jumping on the trampoline, if you get my drift. Lyrically, it said little else. I can't imagine that in heaven we were going to sing songs that promote sexual promiscuity, can you?

Song 7: This song was truly revolting. I could scarcely believe that it was being played on the airwaves. It told the tale of a high school principal having an illicit sexual affair with one of the students. Where is the wisdom in broadcasting this? Is *every* song on the radio these days about extramarital or aberrant sex?

Song 8: This was, I admit, a catchy tune that encouraged listeners to party all night and do whatever they wanted to do. Life "ain't nothing but a party," was the clear message. When taken to heart, that message will rob many a young person of a prosperous and/or fulfilling life. The Bible speaks clearly against licentious living and the pain it causes: Christians ought to avoid glorifying it.

There were more songs, but I'm sure I have made my point. Sinful human beings sing songs that dwell on heartbreak, licentiousness, misery, adultery, violence and many other unpleasant things God tried to spare us from when He gave us the Ten Commandments. Heaven weeps over the pain and suffering that sin has caused; it is hard to imagine the angels entertaining themselves with songs about it. Why should Christians participate in the practice?

There was one refrain in the last song that I found particularly striking:

> Have a good time, lay back and relax
> Just free your mind
> Let the music take control of you.

Could it be true? Does music actually control us? Can it really alter the way we think?

I have met many Christians who roll their eyes when the subject of objectionable music comes up, arguing that tones and percussive sounds are indifferent to moral standards. To many Christians, music is simply a matter of taste; it cannot be considered good or evil.

Frankly that's a little naïve. A musical tone may be morally neutral, but how it's used certainly is not. For example, a framing hammer is neither good nor evil, but if I hit you over the head with it, it becomes a powerful vehicle for an immoral act.

Music is a powerful vehicle for conveying ideas; so powerful, in fact, that during World War II the American government sponsored a study of its effects on human behavior and emotion. One of the researchers, Dr. Ira Altshuler, points out:

> Music, which does not depend on the master brain to gain entrance into the organism, can still arouse by way of the thalamus—the relay station of all emotions, sensations, and feelings. Once a stimulus has been able to reach the thalamus, the master brain is automatically invaded.[90]

Do you know what I find utterly amazing? Generally speaking, I have found that it's *only Christians* who deny that music affects the way you think. I'm not alone in this observation. Christian music professor Tim Fisher, in *The Battle for Christian Music,* makes this observation:

> Those who have looked beyond the current music publications know that no one has ever taken the position that music is neutral except for Christians in the last twenty-five years...[91]

Many Christians deny it, but the rest of the world acknowledges it and uses it! Throughout history, music has been central to almost any successful propaganda campaign. Both Hitler and Stalin used it to help change the way their subjects thought, and millions died.

Carefully think it through; why is it that movie makers will pay hundreds of thousands of dollars to have music written for their movies? It's because music changes the way you think and the way you evaluate information. Take the scary music out of a suspense film, and suddenly it's not half as frightening. Take away the sappy sentimental music, and something is changed; you're not as likely to be moved to tears when Timmy finds Lassie or when Sally finds her true love, without the orchestra track priming your emotions. Movies or television programs with little music seem less engaging.

Why is it that people who write commercials almost always set them to music? It's because it is far easier to plant an idea into our subconscious that way. You will remember it. How often do you catch yourself humming the tune from a television commercial? More often than you'd like to admit, I will bet. See if you can finish these sentences:

1. McDonalds—we do it...
2. Plop, plop, fizz, fizz, oh what a...
3. Tweet, tweet, twiddle, twiddle, there's only one candy with the hole...

Chances are, unless you've been living in a cave, you were able to complete at least one of those sentences, if not all of them. Yet those jingles are all at least 20 years old! You remember them because they were *musical*, and they were quickly and permanently sealed in your memory banks because of it. Advertisers capitalize on the fact that music is a powerful vehicle for embedding an idea into your mind.

No one was more aware of this than rock legend Jimi Hendrix who said: *I can explain everything better through music. You can hypnotize people with music and when you get them at their weakest point, you can preach into their subconscious whatever you want to say.*[92]

Personally, I would like to know with certainty what's being preached into my subconscious, because the human mind is the battleground on which Christ and Satan are fighting for our allegiance. It is critical to be certain about the ideas being fostered there. The enemy of souls is deliberately trying to load faulty information into our computers.

I like to think of the mind as a filing cabinet. I realize that's not a strictly clinical analogy, but I think it works. Day after day, year after year, we drop information into our minds and file it away for a time when we might need it. When faced with a crisis situation, we quickly dip into the filing cabinet to find something to help us make a wise decision. If the information is corrupt, we are going to do the wrong thing.

As the generation that produced rock music grows older, we can no longer claim that rock 'n' roll is the exclusive domain of teenagers. Young people remain particularly susceptible to its dubious charms, however. It has been estimated that the average teenager will listen to more than 11,000 hours of popular rock music between the seventh and twelfth grades, which is more than twice as much time as they'll spend in class.[93] How much of the information that they're picking up from all that music is going to help them make wise life choices?

Christians ought to be aware. There is no question that music is a powerful informational vehicle. Over time, it can literally change the way you think. Once the "ear-gate" has willingly been opened, ideas can slip into your filing cabinet that you might not want there.

We should remind ourselves more often that Lucifer is a musical angel. The Bible indicates that he may have worked in heaven's music department by mentioning that he was created with "timbrels" and "pipes:"

"You were in Eden, the garden of God; every precious stone was your covering: the sardius, topaz, and diamond, beryl, onyx, and jasper, sapphire, turquoise, and emerald with gold. The workmanship of your timbrels and pipes was prepared for you on the day you were created." (Ezekiel 28:13)

One thing is certain: Lucifer has studied and understood the subject of music for much longer than we have. He understands rather well that his rebellious ideas can easily be implanted into our minds. Over time, as we listen to the wrong things, we begin to think like him.

Some years ago, pop singer Barry Manilow performed a hit song that tells a bit of a tale on the music industry. See if you can figure out who or what this song is singing about:

> I've been alive forever
> And I wrote the very first song.
> I put the words and the melodies together,
> I am the music, and I write the songs.
> I write the songs that make the whole world sing.
> My home lies deep within you,
> And I've got my place in your soul.
> Now when I look out through your eyes,
> I'm young again, even though I'm very old.[94]

Who is this song about? It may well be a simple coincidence that the words sound so ominous, and I doubt that the author was thinking of the devil when he wrote the song. But, given the Bible's description of Lucifer's timbrels and pipes, something tells me that this is more than mere coincidence.

If you listen carefully to the product of the rock industry, you'll be able to hear a fallen angel singing. Some famous rock personalities are willing to admit it. For example, the legendary Little Richard states:

> My true belief about Rock 'n' Roll is this: I believe this kind of music is demonic…A lot of the beats in music today are taken from voodoo, from the voodoo drums.[95]
>
> I was directed and commanded by another power. The power of darkness…the power of the devil. Satan.[96]
>
> Rock 'n' Roll doesn't glorify God. You can't drink out of God's cup and the devil's cup at the same time. I was one of the pioneers of that music, one of the builders. I know what the blocks are made of because I built them.[97]

Frankly, it's hard for Christians to ignore testimony like this. Not everything you listen to is good for you. There are dark forces at work that are interested in corrupting your moral database. So, what are *you* listening to?

---

[90] Ira Altshuler, "A psychiatrist's Experiences with Music as a Therapeutic Agent," *Music and Medicine* (New York, 1948), p. 170.

[91] Tim Fisher, *The Battle for the Christian Mind,* (Sacred Music Services, 1992)

[92] *Life Magazine,* October 3, 1969, p. 39.

[93] American Academy of Pediatrics, in Eric Holmberg, *The Power of Music,* www.forerunner.com

[94] *I Write the Songs,* lyrics and music by Bruce Johnston. For more information visit: http://en.wikipedia.org/wiki/I_Write_the_Songs

[95] Charles White, *Life and Times of Little Richard* (Da Capo Press, 1994), p. 197.

[96] Ibid., p. 205.

[97] *Dallas Morning News,* October 29, 1978, p. 14A.

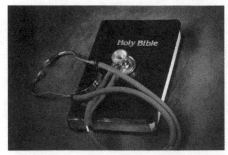

CHAPTER ELEVEN

Mental Health: Television and Movies

Who's Raising Your Kids?

It was a landmark case. Ironically, it was also the first televised trial in American history. In 1977, 15-year-old Ronnie Zamora of Florida took a gun, broke into his neighbor's house, and robbed her. Before he left, 82-year-old Elinor Haggart was dead. With $415 of her money in his hand, Ronnie went on a spending spree with a friend at Disney World.

At his trial, Ronnie's lawyer tried to argue that Ronnie couldn't help himself because he was suffering from something he called "involuntary subliminal television intoxication." His argument was that Ronnie had watched so many violent episodes of programs like "Kojak" that he no longer was able to distinguish between right and wrong.

The court rejected the argument as absurd, and handed Ronnie a life sentence. Yet the question still haunts parents today. What effect does all that TV really have on your kids? For that matter, what effect does all that TV have on *you*?

Like it or lump it, television sets are permanent fixtures in most of our homes. Ninety-nine percent of homes have one, and it's turned on for an average of about 22 hours a week, or just over three hours a day. According to Paul Kropp in a recent issue of *Today's Parent*, children are watching an average of 2.7 hours of TV every single day.[98] That's more time than they spend going to church or talking to their parents! In fact, the U. S. Department of Education estimates that 81 percent of kids under the age of seven have no supervision at all when they watch TV.[99]

In 1977, Ronnie Zamora's lawyer tried to suggest that too much TV turned Ronnie into a murderer. He told the court that Ronnie had unwittingly been conditioned by television programs to rob and kill his neighbor. Ronnie could not be considered a cold-blooded murderer; he was rather to be pitied as the victim of involuntary "television intoxication."

He had lived in a TV fantasy world for so long that he no longer had a grip on reality. For this reason the lawyer entered a plea of "not guilty by reason of insanity."

The court didn't buy it. When Ronnie finally came up for parole in February 2002, he was turned down. The public, it seems, has a little trouble swallowing "TV conditioning" as a defense against murder charges.

Does that mean that television-viewing habits have nothing to do with character formation? Not at all. The court, it should be noted, didn't argue that TV doesn't have a formative role in children's behavioral patterns; it simply argued that Ronnie knew enough to be held accountable for his actions.

The Christian church (as well as other religious groups) has traditionally held that the television industry, as a whole, has been a negative influence on standards of the North American community at large.

Perhaps it's a little naïve to assume that the modern entertainment industry can be blamed for all of society's immorality; but certainly, the industry has to accept *some* responsibility. There's no question that it has left its mark on our otherwise cultured civilization. As many as eighty percent of Hollywood executives admit that they believe there is a link between TV violence and real violence.[100] When you consider that children's programming has been estimated to portray more than twenty violent episodes each hour—four times as many as adult programming[101]—you have got to wonder if young developing minds can really come away unscathed.

The medical and psychiatric communities have little doubt regarding this issue. In January of 2001, U. S. Surgeon General, David Satcher, issued a report describing a demonstrable link between aggressive behavior in children and repeated exposure to violent entertainment.[102] Almost concurrently, the Federal Trade commission released a report proving that the movie industry deliberately markets violent, R-rated movies to kids as young as twelve years of age. Evidence in the report included a memorandum from a Hollywood studio, in which the producers of an R-rated movie stated, "Our goal was to find the elusive teen target audience and make sure everyone between the ages of 12 and 18 was exposed to the film."[103] A marketing plan for another R-rated movie stated that it "seems to make sense to interview 10 and 11 year olds."[104] In other words, inappropriate content is deliberately used as bait for young minds.

Weigh the evidence with me for a moment; the average child witnesses something like 16,000 murders on TV before he reaches the age of 18.[105] Admittedly, that's not new information—we have been hearing those types of statistics for years. But what impact is that level of exposure to violence having on us? A report of the American Senate Judiciary Committee claims that as many as ten percent of youth offenses in the United States can be directly linked to TV viewing.[106]

What you see really *does* affect you. For years the entertainment industry has brushed aside their responsibility in the lowering moral standards of the community, claiming that undesirable content in television programming is simply an honest reflection of society at large. In other words, low societal standards lead to low entertainment standards, not the other way around.

Not everybody in the TV industry agrees. Pat Sajak, the host of *Wheel of Fortune,* said this of the "we're only reflecting reality" argument:

> Television people have put blinders on, and they absolutely refuse—and movie people too—to admit that they can have any influence for ill in our society. You know the argument: "We only reflect what's going on; we don't perpetuate it." And yet not a week goes by in this town where there's not

an award ceremony where they're patting each other on the back, saying, "You raised AIDS awareness" [or] "There'll be no more child abuse thanks to the fine show you did." The argument is you can only influence for good; you can't influence for ill. That makes no sense at all.[107]

I agree. The entertainment industry can't have it both ways. Either what you show on television influences the way people think, or it doesn't. The Bible indicates that it does:

But we all, with unveiled face, beholding as in a mirror the glory of the Lord, are being transformed into the same image from glory to glory, just as by the Spirit of the Lord. (2 Corinthians 3:18)

The spiritual principle Paul is discussing is this: over time, you become more like the things you behold. If you focus your thoughts continually on Jesus Christ, you gradually become more like Him. The more time you spend studying the Bible, the more Christ-like you become and the more resistant you become to temptation. David said in Psalm 119:11, "Your word I have hidden in my heart, that I might not sin against You!"

Good thoughts breed good character. However, the reverse is also true; when you allow your mind to dwell on immorality and violence you gradually alter your value system and become more like the people you're watching. You start to lose you inhibitions. Activities that used to be objectionable or distasteful start to seem acceptable or even desirable. That is why Solomon warns us:

Keep your heart with all diligence, for out of it spring the issues of life. (Proverbs 4:23)

In other words, what you put into your mind (heart) has a direct bearing on the things you allow yourself to say and do. Jesus concurs; your behavior has everything to do with what you feed your mind:

"A good man out of the good treasure of his heart brings forth good things, and an evil man out of the evil treasure brings forth evil things." (Matthew 12:35)

In years past, Christians shunned the theatre as a place that promoted poor morals. It was widely understood that the "treasures of the heart" portrayed on the silver screen were generally of a poor moral quality. Today, however, Christians have few qualms about lining up for the latest box office hit along with everyone else. Have entertainment standards improved so much in the last couple of decades that we no longer need to feel threatened? Is the theater morally purer now than it was a few of generations ago?

Hardly. If past generations of churchgoers thought that most Hollywood movies appeal to our baser instincts, they would roll over in their graves if they could see what Christians are paying to see today. Standards have slipped deep into the gutter. There are more reasons today than ever for Christians to shun the movie theaters.

"Wait a minute. Christians might not go to the theater, but they're hypocrites. They watch the same stuff at home on their TV's!"

I have heard that argument a thousand times. Frankly, I can't argue with it. It's true. Many Christians watch the same TV shows and rent or buy the same movies as everyone else, thinking nothing of it. Apparently, the devil knew that if he couldn't get the Christian to come to the silver screen, he could always bring the silver screen to the Christian.

Although it is painful to admit it, I am becoming increasingly aware of an increasing lack of discernment among modern Christians. I am disturbed by the growing number of Christian wives, from all walks of life and denominations, who come to me to complain that their church-going husbands watch pornographic films or look at pornographic material on the Internet.[108] A recent study I stumbled across made my hair stand on end: more than one-half of Christians staying in a hotel for a religious convention some years ago were found to order adult movies in their rooms.[109]

Not every example is as extreme as that. I recently asked a church youth group what the most popular show on television was. They all knew the answer; it was a program about teenage sex. Admittedly, it's becoming very hard to *not* know such things, but the group was a little too familiar with the program for my comfort. Not only did they know the name of the program, they also knew what time it aired and on which stations. They also knew the names of the actors, and could recite the plots of most episodes.

Next, I asked them which book of the Bible the story of David and Goliath is found in. I didn't ask for chapter and verse, just the book. In addition, they were allowed to flip through their Bibles and look for it. The room fell quiet. Nobody knew. Some awkwardly thumbed through their Bibles, but were unable to find it.

I wonder how many adults would fare any better.

Let's pause for a moment of honest self-examination. Are you more familiar with your TV guide than you are with the Word of God?

A few years ago I had the privilege of meeting Dr. Ben Carson, the world famous pediatric neurosurgeon. A group of us listened to him speak about the wonders of the human brain. "If I were to bring somebody into this room," he said, "and let them look it over for just a couple of seconds, I could produce vivid memories of it 20 years from now by using probes to stimulate specific areas in the brain. They would be able to remember where you sat, what you were wearing, and even what time it was on the clock at the back of the room."[110]

His lecture that evening made a strong impression on my wife and me. Getting ready for bed that night, we talked about what we had heard. "Just think," Jean said, "everything you ever see is in your mind *forever.* Think about all the TV people watch!"

She's right. Everything you witness with your eyes is filed somewhere in your mind forever. It is a permanent record. Most North American kids have 200,000 violent acts filed away in their permanent record by the time they turn 18,[111] and still we shake our heads and wonder why the classroom and schoolyard have become so violent.

A few years ago researchers at the University of Michigan studied the effects of frightening movies and television programs on the human mind. They discovered that, in addition to creating short-term anxiety, such films had residual effects that could linger for years:

> "This may not be surprising, but the proportion of participants—one in four—who reported fright effects that they were still experiencing indicates that these responses should be of major concern," says Harrison, UM assistant professor of communication studies. "These effects were

more serious than jumpiness at a slammed door or the need to use a nightlight. They ranged from an inability to sleep through the night for months after exposure to steadfast and continuing avoidance of the situations portrayed in the programs and movies.

The researchers…found that 52 percent of the sample reported disturbances in normal behavior such as sleeping or eating after viewing a frightening film or TV program. More than a third avoided or dreaded the depicted situation in their own lives and nearly a fourth reported obsessive thinking or talking about the frightening stimulus.

While more than a fourth of the study's participants still experience such aftermath, the duration of the effects—both past and present—range from less than a week (about 33 percent of the sample) to more than a year (36 percent).

According to the study, a wide range of symptoms were reported, including crying or screaming (27 percent of the participants), trembling or shaking (24 percent), nausea or stomach pain (20 percent), clinging to a companion (18 percent), increased heart rate (18 percent), freezing or feeling of paralysis (17 percent), and fear of losing control (11 percent), as well as sweating, chills or fever, fear of dying, shortness of breath, feeling of unreality, dizziness or faintness, and numbness (all less than 10 percent each.)"[112]

I first heard about this study shortly after it was released, on a radio broadcast during which someone stated that these adverse effects can literally go on for many years after a person has watched the film, disturbing healthy sleep patterns. That is not hard to believe, because everything that ever goes into your mind stays there. It is permanent; you keep it. It becomes a part of who you are. No wonder King David made this pledge:

I will behave wisely in a perfect way. Oh, when will You come to me? I will walk within my house with a perfect heart. I will set nothing wicked before my eyes; I hate the work of those who fall away; It shall not cling to me. (Psalm 101:2, 3)

There is nothing new under the sun. David may not have had satellite TV, but there was sill plenty of smut to go around in his world. Today, the filth is much more prevalent, and some Christians seem less committed to guarding the eye-gate than David was.

Does this mean Christians should never watch TV? Of course not. *It Is Written* is on TV, and so are many other good Christian programs. I freely admit that I enjoy my television set when I watch it. But I'm very careful about what I allow into my home and into my mind. Jean and I are doubly careful about what kinds of programming we expose our children to.[113]

Information flashes by so quickly on TV that your frontal lobe—the portion of your brain you use to make moral judgments and decisions—simply doesn't have time to keep up. Because the stream of information is simply too much to process, your mind starts to drop information into your subconscious "filing cabinet" without attaching any moral judgment to it. That information then becomes part of your permanent body of knowledge.

Perhaps you remember Janet Leigh, the actress who starred in Alfred Hitchcock's bone-chilling *Psycho*. The most famous scene in that movie was that of a woman being stabbed to death in the shower. When you mention *Psycho,* most people can remember screeching violin strings and blood running silently down the drain. (We remember it because it's stored in our memory *forever*!)

What many people don't know about *Psycho* is the effect it had on Janet Leigh herself. A few years ago I watched a TV interview in which she confessed that she still has trouble taking a shower to this day. I have since then seen her admission in print:

> "It's true that I don't take showers. If there is no other way to bathe, then I make sure that all the doors and window in the house are locked, and I leave the bathroom door open and the shower curtain or stall door open so I have a perfect, clear view. I face the door no matter where the showerhead is."[114]

From the moment the shower curtain is ripped back, through the staccato shots of knife and flesh, to the blood swirling down the drain and the close-up of Leigh's pinpoint pupils as she lay lifeless on the bathroom floor, the scene has gripped audiences like few others.

Leigh said she is proud of the lasting impression that the scene, and the movie overall, has left in the popular imagination, and acknowledged that moviegoers who were left fearful of taking a shower are in good company.

> "I do not take showers," she said. "As a result of seeing it edited, or put together, it left such an indelible impression on my mind that I cannot take a shower. And that is the truth."[115]

If it had that kind of effect on somebody on *that* side of the camera, what effect does have on those of us on *this* side of the camera? Scores of people continue to tell Janet Leigh that they still lock the doors before they shower because of a film they saw over 40 years ago.

Are you still not convinced that what you watch affects the way you think? Then consider this: How can the television industry charge an average of $2.6 million for a 30-second commercial during the Super Bowl?[116] It's because corporations know for certain what some of us are loathe to admit—what you see on TV really *can* change the way you think. They are willing to pay millions because they are certain that just 30 seconds of exposure will buy them enough business to make it worth it. Some companies have been known to pay nearly $200,000 for a 30-second spot during the educational programs shown in schools, knowing that they have a captive audience of millions of students who will become customers.[117]

Christians ought to be wary; if seconds of exposure can persuade us to change brands, couldn't the thousands of hours of programming we watch persuade us to change some of our moral values?

A growing number of parents are starting to sense it might be true. Special interest groups are on the rise, and investigations of the industry and it's standards are taking place at the highest levels of government. In Canada, 200,000 Canadians decided that something had to be done after Mark Lapine massacred 14 female students in the 1989 Montreal massacre. They petitioned the Canadian Radio Television and Telecommunications Commission (CRTC) to do something about the level of TV violence that families are being subjected to. In 1991 a brave 13-year-old girl from Quebec, who was convinced that TV violence had something to do with the rape and murder of her little sister, started a petition to put a stop to it. By the time Virginie Lariviere presented her petition to Prime Minister Brian Mulroney it had more than 1.3 million Canadian signatures.[118] People have had enough.

In addition to the gratuitous violence routinely portrayed on television, the constant portrayal of low moral standards has also taken its toll on our families and society. Primetime TV programs are riddled with sexual innuendo that would have caused our forefathers to blush just a generation ago. Even though parent groups have been protesting loudly, a study conducted at Southern Illinois University revealed that the frequency of indecent language during primetime programming increased 45 percent between 1990 and 1994.[119] It continues to rise.

Daytime talk shows are just as bad, making a spectacle out of aberrant and promiscuous lifestyles. The lineup of topics would have shocked those living just a generation ago. A report in *Policy Review* a few years ago offered a few samples of what's currently available on daytime television. These are actual topics:[120]

Jenny Jones (Warner Bros. Television). Guests have included: a woman who said she got pregnant while making a pornographic movie, and a husband who had been seeing a prostitute for two years and whose wife confronted him on the show. *Selected show titles:* "A mother who ran off with Her Daughter's Fiancé," "Women Discuss their Sex Lives with their Mothers."

Sally Jessy Raphael (Multimedia Entertainment). Guests have included: a 13-year-old girl who was urged to share her sexual experiences beginning at age 10; a person who claimed to have slept with over 200 sexual partners; a man who appeared on stage with roses for the daughter he had sexually molested, and revealing that he had been molested when he was five. *Selected show titles:* "Sex Caught on Tape," "My Daughter is Living as a Boy," "Wives of Rapists," "I'm Marrying a 14-year-old Boy."

Jerry Springer (Multimedia Entertainment). Guests have included: a man who admitted to sleeping with his girlfriend's mother; a 16-year-old girl (wearing sunglasses to disguise her identity) who said she buried her newborn baby alive in her backyard; a 17-year-old who had married her 71-year-old foster father (with whom she first had sex when she was 14) and had borne him four children; a husband who revealed to his wife on the show that he was having an affair, after which the mistress emerged, kissed the husband, and told the wife that she loved them both.

Montel Williams (Paramount). Guests have included: a pregnant woman who boasted of having eight sexual partners during her first two trimesters; a 17-year-old girl who boasted of having slept with more than a hundred men; a man claiming to be an HIV-positive serial rapist of prostitutes. *Selected show titles:* "Married Men who Have Relationships with the Next-Door Neighbor," "Promiscuous Teenage Girls."

Maury Povich (Paramount). Guests have included: a young mother who had no qualms about leaving her sons in the care of her father, a convicted child molester, because the father had only molested girls.

I could go on, but I am sure the point has been made. It is hard to believe that just a couple of generations ago Lucille Ball was prohibited by censors from using the word "pregnant" on TV because it was considered too risqué. One media analyst has pointed out that the average viewer now sees more sex between strangers than married people on TV:

> Has the world of television prime time become more sexual over time? According to media content analysis conducted by the Center of Media and Public Affairs

(CMPA), prior to 1969 fewer than one instance of extramarital sex was coded for every 30 shows. During the early 1970s, extramarital sex cropped up on about one of every eight shows. Since the mid 1970s, the ratio has dropped to one in six, and continues to narrow.

And not coincidentally, standards of sexual morality have changed just as dramatically. Prior to 1970, 38 percent of the shows coded by CMPA presented extramarital sex as wrong. The proportion dropped to only seven percent after 1970. In the 1970s and 1980s, 41 percent of prime time shows coded viewed recreational sex as acceptable without qualification, and 33 percent made no moral judgment. Currently, 94 percent of sexual encounters presented in soap operas involve unmarried individuals.[121]

I wonder. What message does that kind of programming give our kids?

Jesus warned us that it's not just committing adultery that is a sin—so is wishing you could do it. "But I say to you," said Jesus in Matthew 5: 28, "that whoever looks at a woman to lust for her has already committed adultery with her in his heart." I wonder what He would have to say about a society that watches adultery and sexually explicit material for entertainment. What effect is it having on our supposedly Christian minds—and what effect is it having on our children? Studies show that the average parent spends only 38.5 minutes in meaningful conversation with their children every week, but sits in front of the TV for more than 20 hours a week.[122]

Whose values are your children *really* growing up with?

We keep pills locked in the medicine cabinet because we don't want kids to find them. We watch our children like a hawk at the beach because we don't want them to drown. We teach them to look both ways before they cross the street, and we warn them never to accept rides from strangers. But at the same time, we let the television networks educate them for 20 hours or more a week, and 81 percent of the time we are not paying attention to what they are being taught.

Sex and violence aren't the only challenges TV presents to the family. Another significant problem is the amount of advertising your children are subjected to when they are glued to the tube. The average child will see 20,000 television commercials a year that are specifically designed to change their values.[123]

Advertisers target young children because they understand that children develop loyalty to specific products at a very young age. Recent studies by the National Institute on Media and the Family indicate that children develop brand loyalty as young as two years of age.

What effect does all the propaganda have on our children? For that matter, what effect does it have on you? It has been estimated that by the time you reach 65 years of age, you will have watched two million commercials,[124] every one of which was specifically designed to make you want something you don't have.

Yet the Bible warns us against something called *covetousness*. Jesus says in Luke 12:15, "…Take heed and beware of covetousness, for one's life does not consist in the abundance of the things he possesses."

The apostle Paul wrote in Philippians 4:11, "…I have learned, in whatever state I am, to be content."

The TV advertising industry, on the other hand—grossing somewhere around $40 billion a year[125]—continues to persuade us that the more we have, the happier we will be. We are being taught to be *discontent* in whatever state we are in!

Our addiction to entertainment can take a toll on our physical health too, by encouraging us to be more sedentary.

It has been demonstrated that men who watch more than 21 hours of TV each week double their risk of becoming diabetic.[126] In addition to that, junk food manufacturers are one of the heaviest advertisers during children's programming, promoting unhealthy dietary habits. Children who spend 20 hours a week in front of the television aren't getting any exercise.

It's a recipe for disaster. In fact, almost one-third of American children with diabetes have adult-onset type 2 diabetes because of lifestyle and diet.[127] Turning off the tube might be a great way to help prevent your kids from getting it.

It would also be a great way to help improve their minds. According to a study done by the U.S. Department of Education, academic achievement drops sharply for children who watch more than 10 hours of TV a week.[128] In a number of studies across the continent, it has been conclusively proven that kids who watch a lot of TV scored lower on reading, writing and math tests.[129]

Is that a coincidence? Not at all. Across North America we sign out twice as many videos as library books. Are the shows our kids watch educational? The Annenburg Public Policy Center estimated in 2000 that as many as 21 percent of self-professed educational programs directed at children have no real educational value.

On top of that, some researchers are now suggesting that there may be a link between the amounts of TV a child watches before age five and the likelihood that he or she will develop attention deficit disorder.[130] While the studies are not as yet conclusive, there is a considerable body of evidence to suggest that once the neural pathways of a small child have been conditioned to receive information from a fast-moving, attention-grabbing television show, the teacher has a tough time competing with just a piece of chalk and a chalkboard.

What am I suggesting? Should we pack up everything and go back to the Dark Ages? No. Personally, I like some of the technological advances we have made. I like to be able to check the news and weather on my satellite receiver. I like the fact that I can listen to some of my favorite preachers from around the world. I like to be able to log onto the Internet and find the information I need without having to go down to the library. I am not ready to go back to the Dark ages, and I am not suggesting it for anybody else, either.

Many preachers over the years have suggested that everybody throw out their TV sets, but I don't recommend that step, unless you find that you simply cannot practice any self-control. In that case, it is better to get rid of it. (If you're going to throw out your TV, let me know where you throw it!)

I'm not even sure more censorship is the solution, even though I pray that the people responsible for programming would develop a stronger conscience and think twice about what they are sending into our homes.

(After all, they must live in the society they're polluting, too.) I am leery of imposing the kind of tight controls that would establish a monstrosity little better than the unholy marriage between church and state that precipitated the Inquisition.

Here is one thing I *am* suggesting, however, and it's remarkably simple; Christians could exercise more discretion. The consumer is just as guilty as the producer when it comes to propagating filth on TV. It's time to stop letting those who don't seem to have any real moral principles set the standard for our families. It's also time to be honest and admit that if we didn't have such a voracious appetite for violence and smut, the network producers wouldn't be putting it on the air.

What would happen if we simply refused to watch it? Once Hollywood felt the economic pinch, they might smarten up. Perhaps we would have more time for the Word of God, too.

You really *do* have a choice. You could turn the "idiot box" off more often. We don't have to allow vulgarity to triumph in our homes. Your children might not thank you for it right now, but one day, when they have grown up and they have got healthy minds and healthy families of their own, they will.

The Bible makes it very clear what our standards should be:

Finally, brethren, whatever things are true, whatever things are noble, whatever things are just, whatever things are pure, whatever things are lovely, whatever things are of good report, if there is any virtue and if there is anything praiseworthy—meditate on these things. (Philippians 4:8)

———————————

[8] Paul Kropp, "TV or Not TV," *Today's Parent*, September 1999.

[99] US Department of Education, "Strong Families, Strong Schools: Building Community Partnerships for Learning" (report), 1994.

[100] "Facts and Figures about our TV Habit," *TV Turnoff Network, Real Vision,* Fact Sheet. A copy may be viewed at www.tv.turnoff.org; accessed January 2003.

[101] André Gosselin, et al, "Violence on Canadian Television and Some of Its Cognitive Effects," *Canadian Journal of Communications,* Volume 2, Number 22, 1997.

[102] "Youth Violence: A Report of the Surgeon General," January 2001.

[103] Jessica Portner, "Congress Grills Hollywood Over Marketing Practices," *Education Week,* September 20, 2000.

[104] In Senate Commerce Committee Hearing: Federal Trade Commission Report on Marketing Violent Entertainment to Children, Statement of Senator John McCain, September 13, 2000.

[105] Real Vision fact sheet.

[106] Frank V. York, "Soul Murder: Are Bad Parenting and the Popular Culture Creating a Generation of Psychopaths?" *Family Research council.* A copy is posted at www.frc.org; accessed January 2003.

[107] In Bob Smithouser, "Mind over Media," *Focus on the Family Magazine,* April 2001, p. 7.

[108] I do not wish to mislead the reader; the number of such occasions is not excessive, but as the availability of such materials is becoming more widespread, the problem *is* increasing.

[109] I have deliberately chosen not to reference this, since I found it in a publication that was using this statistic to make a mockery of biblical Christianity, and I have no desire to give them publicity.

[110] I am, of course, paraphrasing Dr. Carson, since I am not able to probe my own brain and produce a literal word-for-word rendition of what he said. My apologies to Dr. Carson if this is not exactly what he said.

[111] Real Vision fact sheet.

[112] University of Michigan, News and Information Services, March 8, 1999 News Release.

[113] Our children, at the time of writing, are quite young. As a result they watch very little television. There is mounting evidence to suggest that television viewing has adverse effects on psychological development in children under five, and that it's best to keep them away from the TV set all together. The American Pediatric Association recommends absolutely no TV before the age of two. You might be interested in checking out some of the materials available at www.limitv.org.

[114] Elaine Ward, *Once Upon a Parable,* (Educational Ministries), 1994, p. 8.

[115] "Janet Leigh Returns to Bates Motel to enact *Psycho* Scene," Reuters, August 3, 2000.

[116] Cost for a 30-second commercial according to *The New York Times,* January 5, 2007.

[117] Center for Commercial-Free Public Education, "Channel One." www.commercialfree.org/channelone.html; accessed January 2003.

[118] "Television Violence: Fraying our Social Fabric," *Report of the House of Commons Standing Committee on Communication and Culture,* June 1993.

[119] Senator Joseph Lieberman, "Why Parents Hate TV," *Policy Review* (Heritage Foundation: May-June 1996), Number 77.

[120] Ibid. This list of topics is taken from Senator Lieberman's study.

[121] Robert Lichter, "Sex and Television Programming," *Testimony of David Murray, Ph.D, before Senate Subcommittee on Oversight of Government Management, Restructuring, and the District of Columbia, of the Committee on Governmental Affairs,* May 8, 1997.

[122] Real Vision fact sheet.

[123] Ibid.

[124] Ibid.

[125] Ibid.

[126] Ibid.

[127] Ibid.

[128] US Department of Education, "Strong Families, Strong Schools, Building Community Partnerships for Learning," 1994.

[129] See www.limitv.org; accessed January 2003.

[130] See http://www.limitv.org/tvaddadhd.htm; accessed March 2002.

CHAPTER TWELVE

Mental Health: Changing Habits

How to Get Out of Ruts

Have you ever done anything that you really didn't want to do? Was it last week, yesterday, or maybe even today? I certainly have. Why is it that we are constantly doing things we don't want to do—or know we shouldn't be doing? This is one of the biggest frustrations of life.

A number of years ago when I (Fred Hardinge) was in graduate school, each student was assigned a mailbox. This was before the days of email and personal computers. The mailbox was the place where students picked up their graded papers and assignments and where teachers and students communicated with each other. It was very important to check that box several times a day.

I walked by that box when I went to school, between classes, and on my way home. Even on weekends I would sometimes pass by and check it. I did this for more than three years. Then I graduated and moved to the other side of the country. I no longer had to check the mailbox.

It was probably 15 years later that I returned to the same graduate school to attend some continuing education classes. I will never forget what happened. It was about mid-morning on the first day of classes, and I was walking with two of my colleagues from one classroom to another. We were deep in conversation about the presentation we had just heard,

117

when our route turned the corner of the hallway, and there to my right was that old bank of mailboxes. Without even thinking—and in mid-sentence—I looked right and checked the old box!

This is something I had not done in all the intervening years since graduation. Both of my professional colleagues gave me the strangest looks, too. Why did I look into the box without even thinking about what I was doing? That's right. During all those years in graduate school I had formed a habit of looking into the box every time I walked past.

What is a habit? Habits are any action—physical, mental, or emotional—that we carry out under a particular set of circumstances without having to consciously think about it. We develop habits by choosing to repeat them over and over again under the same set of circumstances. When we can carry out that particular action without conscious thought, it is a habit.

Are habits good or bad? Of course, they can be either. Habits are the autopilot of our lives. Habits are actually a tremendous blessing to us. They make life efficient. If we did not have the ability to form habits, we would not be able to accomplish very much. You would probably still be tying your shoes, combing your hair, or trying to figure out how to get your car out of the driveway safely. (Remember how long it took for your children to learn to tie *their* shoes?)

Many people consider habits to be a curse. That is probably because we take the good ones for granted, and have so much trouble trying to change the bad ones. Bad habits seem to strengthen in bands of steel that entrap us in doing things we really don't want to do.

Whenever we discuss changing habits, there is another closely related concept we need to understand: instinct. What is an instinct? Instincts are habits which an animal or human is born with. To use an illustration from the computer world, they are "built into the hardware."

When my children were small, I picked up one of their newly-born kittens and took it outside in my hand. It meowed and meowed and was not very happy. The children's eyes were wide with wonderment and fear, especially when I called our German shepherd dog that did not like cats. I am sure they thought I was going to feed the kitten to the dog. That, however, was not my intention.

After commanding the dog to sit, I slowly brought the kitten in my outstretched arm closer and closer to the dog's nose. As that little, blind kitten got closer to the dog, her little nose began sniffing new scents. All of a sudden she hissed and spit ferociously. I then pulled my hand back and we took the kitten back to her mother. My children, and the kitten, were greatly relieved!

What made that little kitten respond to our dog's scent as all cats do when they meet a strange dog? Was it a formed habit, or was it instinct? The kitten was born inside our house, and had never even smelled a dog. Yet when confronted by the odor of our dog for the first time in its life, it did what all cats do, because of instinct.

As we understand the fundamental difference between habits and instincts, it gives us fresh insights into God's love. You see, our habits can be changed, but our instincts cannot. All habits are learned—and they all begin with repeated choices we have made under a specific set of circumstances. God never changes us against our choice. And, we never establish or change any habits without choosing to do so first.

Instincts do not involve our power of choice. When we look at the animal world, we recognize that the vast majority of their lives are controlled by their inborn instincts. From the first day of life, kittens exhibit the behavior of cats. Puppies behave like dogs. Young colts act like horses. True, each type of animal can be trained to form some habits, but the greater part of their lives are controlled by their instincts.

What portion of our lives as humans is controlled by instinct? Not very much at all. The vast majority of our lives is controlled by habits— all of which we have chosen to learn. When you think about it carefully, humans are born with very, very few instincts. A newborn kitten can find its way to her mother's milk from a few feet away. However, a young human infant would starve from the same distance.

Because our lives are controlled primarily by habits, praise God we can change! Yet to change is probably the most difficult thing humans ever attempt to accomplish. I believe it is far easier for a human to climb Mt. Everest than it is to naturally change an ingrained habit.

Let's take a look at how habits are formed in our brains. All habits are laid down in the nerve cells of the brain. Extending from each nerve cell are many little fibers called dendrites, and one long fiber called the axon. The dendrites are like miniature receivers that pick up incoming electrochemical messages. The long axon is like a small transmitter that sends messages to neighboring cells.

Many years ago, Sir John Eccles, of Australia, was using a powerful microscope to examine the tiny space between the sending axon of one nerve cell and the receiving dendrites of another cell. He noticed some tiny bumps on the end of the axon that looked to him like miniature buttons; and he called them boutons, which is French for button. Today we know those little boutons on the end of the axon secrete various chemicals that bridge the gap between the cells and allow the transmission of a message from one nerve cell to another.

Dr. Eccles noticed that some axons had many boutons while others had only a few, and that those sending fibers with many boutons did not require as much stimulation as those with few in order to send the impulse on to the next cell. He theorized that boutons might be formed when that particular sending fiber is repeatedly stimulated, thus making it increasingly easier for messages to flow along that particular pathway. More recent research has confirmed this. Under electron microscopes researchers have indeed found that repeated stimulation does cause boutons to enlarge and multiply.

In this way, any thought or action that is often repeated is actually building little boutons on the end of certain nerve fibers so that it becomes easier to repeat the same thought or action under the same set of circumstances. This is the way habits are formed. It is sobering to realize that every thought, every feeling, or every action that is repeated is producing physical and chemical changes in the nerve pathways of our brains—either to bless us or to curse us.

Do these boutons ever disappear if they are not used? Evidence today indicates they do not. How then can we get rid of an old habit and establish a new one if we can't erase the old ones? The answer lies in recognizing that it can be done by laying down new habit pathways that are even stronger than the old ones. It is only by consistently and repeatedly choosing, under a specific set of circumstances, to do something different that we form a new habit. As the new habit pathway becomes stronger, the old pathway weakens, but it does not completely disappear. The toughest part is consistently making the choice to change.

The apostle Paul graphically described this struggle of habit change in Romans 7:15 when he said: "For what I will to do, that I do not practice; but what I hate, that I do" (see also vs. 19). Have you ever felt like this? The very things you want to do you don't, but the things you don't want to do, those are what you do. There is hope, though. Remember, habits are learned actions, and can be replaced by new ones through the same process as in learning the old one.

We can learn much about habits and how to change them from a simple activity that young and old seem to enjoy. Those who have grown up in northern climates know what happens when the first snow gets deep enough to sled down the neighborhood hills. Who has the best ride down the hill; the first sled of the day, or the last sled of the day? The last sled, of course. But, why? The first riders down the hill have to pack the snow with the runners of the sleds. Only when the tracks get hard and icy does the ride really become easy and fun. Sometimes it takes much effort and many trips down the hill to pack the tracks. And all the sleds have to stay in the same track! Each trip down gets easier and easier.

That is very similar to forming a habit. It takes a strong initial effort to get started, and you have to stay in the track. Then each time you are in those particular circumstances it becomes easier to choose the desired action.

After a fun day of sledding, all the sleds are returned to their respective places. If it snows during the night, when the sleds are taken to the top of the hill the next day all the old tracks are covered. Yet if the sleds are put down where the old tracks were made, it doesn't take very long until the ride is fun and fast again. That is the way with habits as well. Under the "new snow" lies the old packed habit pathway!

What is the best way to establish a new track on the sledding hill? Do you start down in the old track and then turn hard on the runners? No, that is a sure way to spill. The best and safest way of starting a new track on the hill is to pick up the sled at the top of the hill and set it down far enough away from the old track that there is no chance you will slide into the old one on the way down. Usually it is like starting all over again. It takes a strong initial effort. This is the way changing habits is also.

One of the greatest evidences of God's love is that he gave to us the privilege of forming and changing habits. He could have made us like robots by programming us through our instincts. Yet, He made us free moral agents with the power to choose, and the ability to form habits by repeatedly making choices under specific sets of circumstances. We change habits by the same method: repeatedly making different choices under the same circumstances. In theory it is easy; in practice it is the hardest thing for us to do.

Because God loves us, He never changes a habit against our will. We must make the choice. The secret of changing habits is the same secret that Paul discovered to get out of his dilemma in Romans 7. Paul knew he could do anything with God—including change **any** habit! He said, "I can do all things through Christ who strengthens me" Philippians 4:13.

"Just say No" did not originate with Nancy Reagan. The Bible records:

For the grace of God that brings salvation has appeared to all men, teaching us that, denying ungodliness and worldly lusts, we should live soberly, righteously, and godly in the present age. (Titus 2:11,12)

It is God, and only God, who can permanently keep us from falling back into old habits.

Now to Him who is able to keep you from stumbling, And to present you faultless Before the presence of His glory with exceeding joy. (Jude 1:24)

We do not have to rely on our own strength. In fact, if we do, we will almost always fail. The Bible says, "For the weapons of our warfare *are* not carnal but mighty in God for pulling down strongholds…bringing every thought into captivity to the obedience of Christ" (2 Corinthians 10:4-5). What a blessing to be able to rely on the grace and strength of Jesus. All we have to do is choose to consent and cooperate with God.

General Jonathan "Skinny" Wainwright IV was in charge of United States forces in the Philippines at the time of surrender to the Japanese during World War II. Eventually he was captured and became a prisoner of war. He was transported to a POW (prisoner of war) camp somewhere in Manchuria. When the war was over, he and other American servicemen were still being held. One day they heard the drone of American airplane motors. All rushed to the fences to catch a glimpse of the planes, except General Wainwright. He turned and headed to the Japanese commander's office. Without even knocking, he barged right in and stood before the surprised commander and said, "My commander-in-chief has defeated your commander-in-chief. I am in charge here now!"

Each one of us can have victory in Christ through cooperation with Him. When tempted and tried we can look the old devil in the eye and say, "My commander-in-chief, Jesus Christ, defeated you on the cross of Calvary. Jesus is in charge in my life!"

It is the grace of Christ that gives us the power to obey the laws of God. It is this same power that helps us break the bondage of bad habits. This is the only power that can change us into new creatures and keep us in the right path.

You can get out of the rut—through the power of Jesus Christ in your life!

"Thanks be to God, who gives us the victory through our Lord Jesus Christ. Therefore...be steadfast, immovable, always abounding in the work of the Lord." (1 Corinthians 15: 57, 58)

Effective Tools for Changing Habits
1. Choose to make choices, not promises.
2. Make a strong initial effort.
3. Choose a balanced, wholesome lifestyle.
4. Avoid temptations whenever possible.
5. Ask God for help.

CHAPTER THIRTEEN

For Better Health

A Final Word

When we first started to explore what the Bible says about health and well-being, we were astounded at the amount of information it provides. That tells us something important: God values you as a whole person. He cares.

Your body is a delicate instrument, an incredible machine well worth preserving. You only get one mind and one body, and it has got to last you a lifetime. God loves you enough to give you an owner's manual: the Bible.

This little book has explored some basic Bible principles that, when applied conscientiously, will unquestionably add quality to your life. We've hardly had time to scrape the surface, so keep studying! The Bible holds the key to enriching your physical, emotional, spiritual and mental health. When we heed God's counsel in each of these areas, we are bound to enjoy more the abundant life that Christ taught.

Selected Health Resources

The following books and websites are provided by the authors for those looking to delve deeper into some of the topics covered in this book. Unfortunately, space does not allow for an exhaustive list. We wish you a pleasant journey as you discover more steps to a healthier lifestyle.

Exercise
• Nelson, Miriam and Wernick, Sarah. *Strong Women Stay Young*. New York: Bantam Books, 2000. (Excellent book for men also.)
• Energize Your Life: http://www.cdc.gov/nccdphp/dnpa/physical/index.htm. The Centers for Disease Control and Prevention provides a wealth of resources and programs for encouraging you to become physically active.
• Just Move Online: http://www.justmove.org/. This American Heart Association online tool is designed to help people begin or continue being physically active.

Vegetarian Nutrition
• Sabate, Joan, editor; in collaboration with Ratzin-Turner, Rosemary. *Vegetarian Nutrition*. Boca Raton: CRC Press, 2001.
• Messina, Virginia Kisch; Messina, Mark and Mangels, Reed. *The Dietitian's Guide to Vegetarian Diets: Issues and Applications*. Boston: Jones and Bartlett Publishers, 2004.
• Craig, Winston. *Nutrition and Wellness: A Vegetarian Way to Better Health*. Berrien Springs: Golden Harvest Books, 1999.
• Vegetarian Nutrition: http://www.vegetarian-nutrition.info/. A wealth of reliable information on vegetarian nutrition and a healthy lifestyle.
• Nutrition.gov: http://www.nutrition.gov/. An easy to use site providing a host of information on food and human nutrition for consumers.

Tobacco
• Tobacco Information and Prevention Source (TIPS): http://www.cdc.gov/tobacco/. The most comprehensive site on the internet for information about tobacco and its impact on humans.

• Quit Smoking Now Online!: http://www.smokefree.gov/. Find online step-by-step cessation help along with many resources to help you or someone you care about quit smoking.

Alcohol
• Ashton, John F. and Laura, Ronald S. *Uncorked! The Hidden Hazards of Alcohol*. Victoria: Signs Publishing Company, 2004.
• International Commission for the Prevention of Alcoholism and Drug Dependency: http://www.icpaworld.com/. This organization places the spotlight of science on alcoholism and other drug dependencies.

Sleep
• Dement, William C. *The Promise of Sleep*. New York: Delacorte Press, 1999.
• Maas, James B. *Power Sleep: The Revolutionary Program that Prepares Your Mind for Peak Performance*. New York: Villard, 1998.
• Moore-Ede, Martin. *The Twenty-Four-Hour-Society: Understanding Human Limits in a World That Never Stops*. Reading: Addison-Wesley Publishing Company, 1993.
• Sleepless at Stanford: http://www-leland.stanford.edu/~dement/sleepless.html. What everyone should know about how their sleeping lives affect their waking lives.
• SleepNet: http://sleepnet.com/. Everything you wanted to know about sleep but were too tired to ask.
• National Sleep Foundation: http://www.sleepfoundation.org/. Find answers to common questions sleep and fatigue.

Evaluating Health Information
• Guide to Healthy Web Surfing: http://www.nlm.nih.gov/medlineplus/healthywebsurfing.html. Clear and simply guidelines for evaluating the quality of health information on web sites.
• Quackwatch: http://www.quackwatch.org/. A large site providing a guide to quackery, health fraud and how to make intelligent decisions.

It Is Written Resources
• Discover more spiritual resources including: books, music, DVDs, online video programs and Bible studies at: www.itiswritten.com.

Discover Anwers
to life's
Questions

Bibleinfo.com offers answers to hundreds of everyday questions. Discover what the Bible has to say about your question. The answer is only a click away!

KidsBibleinfo.com™
big answers for little people℠

Plus, there is a fun, educational and inspirational site designed for children. Explore interactive games, Bible lessons, character-building stories and more at www.KidsBibleinfo.com.

Bibleinfo.com®

Bible answers to hundreds of life's questions in 17 languages.

Free Bible Guides

A dynamic way to become better acquainted with your Bible.

The DISCOVER BIBLE GUIDES are designed for busy people like you. They will help bring your Bible to life and you can study at home at your own pace. No cost or obligation. Simply mail the coupon below, or call now to begin a new adventure with your Bible. The DISCOVER BIBLE GUIDES are also available online.

IT IS WRITTEN

CALL TODAY

1-800-253-3000

OR LOG ONTO:

www.itiswritten.com

☐ **YES**, please send me the **FREE** *Discover Bible Guides*.

Name _____ Phone _____

Address _____

City _____ State _____ Zip _____

Please mail this coupon to: **It Is Written, Box O, Thousand Oaks, CA 91359**